Async in C# 5.0

Alex Davies

Beijing · Cambridge · Farnham · Köln · Sebastopol · Tokyo

Async in C# 5.0
by Alex Davies

Copyright © 2012 Alex Davies. All rights reserved.
Printed in the United States of America.

Published by O'Reilly Media, Inc., 1005 Gravenstein Highway North, Sebastopol, CA 95472.

O'Reilly books may be purchased for educational, business, or sales promotional use. Online editions are also available for most titles (*http://my.safaribooksonline.com*). For more information, contact our corporate/institutional sales department: 800-998-9938 or *corporate@oreilly.com*.

Editor: Rachel Roumeliotis
Production Editor: Rachel Steely

Cover Designer: Karen Montgomery
Interior Designer: David Futato
Illustrators: Robert Romano and Rebecca Demarest

Revision History for the First Edition:
    2012-09-07   First release
See *http://oreilly.com/catalog/errata.csp?isbn=9781449337162* for release details.

ISBN: 978-1-449-33716-2

[LSI]

1347041598

Table of Contents

Preface

Async is a powerful feature added to the C# programming language in C# 5.0. It comes at a time when performance and parallelization are becoming a major concern of software developers. Used correctly, it can help to write programs with performance and parallelization properties that would have needed reams of code without it. However, what it does to your program is complex, and there are plenty of aspects to how it works that aren't immediately obvious.

Excepting Visual Basic .NET, which added async at the same time as C#, no other mainstream programming languages offer capabilities equivalent to async. Experience and guidance in using it in real-world programs is rare. This book is the guidance from my experience using async, as well as ideas drawn from the designers of C# and computer science theory. More importantly, it shows what async is, how it works, and why you might want to use it.

Intended Audience

This book is intended for people who are already confident C# programmers. Perhaps you are looking to understand async, to choose whether to start using it. Perhaps you have already started using async, but need to learn advanced techniques and caveats to make best use of it.

Having said that, it doesn't assume knowledge of other advanced C# features, so the book is approachable to C# beginners, as well as programmers confident in other languages.

C# is used in many kinds of application, and async is useful for different reasons in each of these. For that reason, this book looks at async from both client and server points of view, including chapters specifically for ASP.NET and WinRT.

How to Read This Book

This book is primarily designed to be read from beginning to end, as a way to learn about async. It introduces concepts in order, helping you to understand with examples before relying on that understanding. This is especially true of the first five chapters of the book.

The best way to learn is by doing, so I recommend that you try out code examples yourself. For this, you'll need a C# development environment, like Microsoft Visual Studio or MonoDevelop. Take opportunities to extend the examples and work on your own programs while reading, to understand the ideas fully.

After reading the book, you may want to go back and use the sixth chapter onwards as a reference for advanced topics in the use of the async. These chapters are organized into self-contained topics.

- Chapters 6 and 7 focus on techniques to use in async code
- Chapters 8 and 9 focus on complex behaviors of async
- Chapters 10 to 13 discuss situations where async is useful
- Chapters 14 and 15 look at how async works internally

Conventions Used in This Book

The following typographical conventions are used in this book:

Italic
> Indicates new terms, URLs, email addresses, filenames, and file extensions.

`Constant width`
> Used for program listings, as well as within paragraphs to refer to program elements such as variable or function names, databases, data types, environment variables, statements, and keywords.

`Constant width italic`
> Shows text that should be replaced with user-supplied values or by values determined by context.

 This icon signifies a tip, suggestion, or general note.

Using Code Examples

This book is here to help you get your job done. In general, you may use the code in this book in your programs and documentation. You do not need to contact us for permission unless you're reproducing a significant portion of the code. For example, writing a program that uses several chunks of code from this book does not require permission. Selling or distributing a CD-ROM of examples from O'Reilly books does require permission. Answering a question by citing this book and quoting example code does not require permission. Incorporating a significant amount of example code from this book into your product's documentation does require permission.

We appreciate, but do not require, attribution. An attribution usually includes the title, author, publisher, and ISBN. For example: "*Async in C# 5.0* by Alex Davies (O'Reilly). Copyright 2012 Alex Davies, 978-1-449-33716-2."

If you feel your use of code examples falls outside fair use or the permission given above, feel free to contact us at *permissions@oreilly.com*.

Safari® Books Online

Safari Books Online (*www.safaribooksonline.com*) is an on-demand digital library that delivers expert content in both book and video form from the world's leading authors in technology and business.

Technology professionals, software developers, web designers, and business and creative professionals use Safari Books Online as their primary resource for research, problem solving, learning, and certification training.

Safari Books Online offers a range of product mixes and pricing programs for organizations, government agencies, and individuals. Subscribers have access to thousands of books, training videos, and prepublication manuscripts in one fully searchable database from publishers like O'Reilly Media, Prentice Hall Professional, Addison-Wesley Professional, Microsoft Press, Sams, Que, Peachpit Press, Focal Press, Cisco Press, John Wiley & Sons, Syngress, Morgan Kaufmann, IBM Redbooks, Packt, Adobe Press, FT Press, Apress, Manning, New Riders, McGraw-Hill, Jones & Bartlett, Course Technology, and dozens more. For more information about Safari Books Online, please visit us online.

How to Contact Us

Please address comments and questions concerning this book to the publisher:

O'Reilly Media, Inc.
1005 Gravenstein Highway North
Sebastopol, CA 95472
800-998-9938 (in the United States or Canada)
707-829-0515 (international or local)
707-829-0104 (fax)

We have a web page for this book, where we list errata, examples, and any additional information. You can access this page at *http://oreil.ly/Async_in_CSharp5*.

To comment or ask technical questions about this book, please send email to *bookquestions@oreilly.com*.

For more information about our books, courses, conferences, and news, see our website at *http://www.oreilly.com.*

Find us on Facebook: *http://facebook.com/oreilly*

Follow us on Twitter: *http://twitter.com/oreillymedia*

Watch us on YouTube: *http://www.youtube.com/oreillymedia*

Acknowledgments

I'd like to thank Stephen Toub for reviewing the book, not just technically, but lending me his experience in getting across parallel computing concepts. His blog was also the first place I saw a lot of the ideas I've explained here. Thank you to Hamish for proofreading, and to Katie for bringing me tea while writing.

Thanks also to Rachel Roumeliotis, my editor, and the team at O'Reilly who have been very helpful while I've been writing.

I thank my family, especially my Mum, who looked after me during the recovery from surgery in which most of the book was written. Finally, I'd like to thank my colleagues at Red Gate, who encouraged the atmosphere of experimentation that led me to learn about async at work.

CHAPTER 1

Introduction

Let's start with a high-level introduction to the *async* feature in C# 5.0, and what it means for you.

Asynchronous Programming

Code is asynchronous if it starts some long-running operation, but then doesn't wait while it's happening. In this way, it is the opposite of blocking code, which sits there, doing nothing, during an operation.

These long-running operations include:

- Network requests
- Disk accesses
- Delays for a length of time

The distinction is all about the *thread* that's running the code. In all widely used programming languages, your code runs inside an operating system thread. If that thread continues to do other things while the long-running operation is happening, your code is asynchronous. If the thread is still in your code, but isn't doing any work, it is blocked, and you've written blocking code.

 Of course, there is a third strategy for waiting for long-running operations, called *polling*, where you repeatedly ask whether the job is complete. While it has its place for very short operations, it's usually a bad idea.

You've probably used asynchronous code before in your work. If you've ever started a new thread, or used the ThreadPool, that was asynchronous programming, because the thread you did it on is free to continue with other things. If you've ever made a web page that a user can access another web page from, that was asynchronous, because there's no thread on the web server waiting for the user's input. That may seem completely obvious, but think about writing a console app that requests the user's input using `Console.ReadLine()`, and you might be able to imagine an alternative blocking design for the web. It may have been a terrible design, yes, but it would have been possible.

The difficulty with asynchronous code is that, quite often, you want to know when an operation is finished. Then you want to do something else. This is trivially easy to do in blocking code: you can just write another line of code below the long-running call. In the asynchronous world, however, this doesn't work, because your next line will almost certainly run before the asynchronous operation has finished.

To solve this, we have invented a menagerie of patterns to run some code after a background operation completes:

- Inserting the code into the background operation, after the main body of the operation
- Signing up to an event that fires on completion
- Passing a delegate or lambda to execute after completion (a *callback*)

If that next operation needs to execute on a particular thread (for example, a *Win-Forms* or *WPF* UI thread), you also need to deal with queuing the operation on that thread. It's all very messy.

What's So Great About Asynchronous Code?

Asynchronous code frees up the thread it was started on. That's really good for lots of reasons. For one thing, threads take up resources on your machine, and using fewer resources is always good. Often, there's only one thread that's able to do a certain job, like the UI thread, and if you don't release it quickly, your app becomes unresponsive. We'll talk more about these reasons in the next chapter.

The biggest reason that I'm excited about async is the opportunity it provides to take advantage of parallel computing. Async makes it reasonable to structure your program in new ways, with much finer-grain parallelism, without the code becoming complicated and unmaintainable. Chapter 10 will explore this possibility.

What Is Async?

In version 5.0 of the C# language, the compiler team at Microsoft has added a powerful new feature.

It comes in the form of two new keywords:

- `async`
- `await`

It also relies on some additions and changes to the .NET Framework 4.5 that power it and make it useful.

 Async is a feature of the C# compiler that couldn't have been implemented by a library. It performs a transformation on your source code, in much the same way that lambdas and iterators do in earlier versions of C#.

The feature makes *asynchronous* programming a lot easier by eliminating the need for complex patterns that were necessary in previous versions of C#. With it, we can reasonably write entire programs in an asynchronous style.

Throughout the book, I'm going to use the term **asynchronous** to refer to the general style of programming that is made easier by the C# feature called **async**. Asynchronous programming has always been possible in C#, but it involved a lot of manual work from the programmer.

What Async Does

The async feature is a way to express what to do after a long-running operation is completed, one that's easy to read but behaves asynchronously.

An async method is transformed by the compiler to make asynchronous code look very similar to its blocking equivalent. Here is a simple blocking method that downloads a web page.

```
private void DumpWebPage(string uri)
{
    WebClient webClient = new WebClient();
    string page = webClient.DownloadString(uri);
    Console.WriteLine(page);
}
```

And here is the equivalent method using async.

```
private async void DumpWebPageAsync(string uri)
{
    WebClient webClient = new WebClient();
    string page = await webClient.DownloadStringTaskAsync(uri);
    Console.WriteLine(page);
}
```

They look remarkably similar. But under the hood, they are very different.

The method is marked async. This is required for any methods that use the await keyword. We've also added the suffix Async to the name of the method, to follow convention.

The interesting bit is the `await` keyword. When the compiler sees this, it chops the method up. Exactly what it does is pretty complicated, so for now I will introduce a false construct that I find useful as a way to think about simple cases.

1. Everything after `await` is moved into a separate method.

2. We use a new version of `DownloadString` called `DownloadStringTaskAsync`. It does the same as the original, but is asynchronous.

3. That means we can give it the new second method, which it will call when it finishes. We do this using some magic that I'll tell you about later.

4. When the download is done, it will call us back with the downloaded `string`—which we can use, in this case, to write to the console.

```
private void DumpWebPageAsync(string uri)
{
    WebClient webClient = new WebClient();
    webClient.DownloadStringTaskAsync(uri) <- magic(SecondHalf);
}

private void SecondHalf(string awaitedResult)
{
    string page = awaitedResult;
    Console.WriteLine(page);
}
```

What happens to the calling thread when it runs this code? When it reaches the call to `DownloadStringTaskAsync`, the download gets started. But not in this thread. In this thread, we reach the end of the method and return. What the thread does next is up to our caller. If it is a UI thread, it will go back to processing user actions. Otherwise, its resources might be released. That means we've written asynchronous code!

Async Doesn't Solve Everything

The async feature has deliberately been designed to look as similar to blocking code as possible. We can deal with long-running or remote operations almost as if they were local and fast, but keep the performance benefits of calling them asynchronously.

However, it's not designed to let you forget that there are background operations and callbacks happening. You need to be careful with lots of things that behave differently when you use async, including:

- Exceptions and try..catch...finally blocks
- Return values of methods
- Threads and context
- Performance

Without understanding what's really happening, your program will fail in surprising ways, and you won't understand the error messages or the debugger to be able to fix it.

CHAPTER 2

Why Programs Need to Be Asynchronous

Asynchronous programming is important and useful, but the reason that it's important varies, depending on what kind of application you're writing. Some of the benefits exist everywhere, but matter most in a kind of application that you may never write. If this applies to you, do read the whole chapter, as the background knowledge will help you to understand the whole context.

Desktop User Interface Applications

Desktop applications have one primary performance requirement. They need to feel responsive to the user. Human Computer Interaction (HCI) studies have shown that users don't notice a slow application, as long as the interface is responsive, and preferably has an animated progress indicator.

People get frustrated with the program when it freezes up. Freezes are usually the result of the program being unable to respond to user input during a long-running operation, whether that's during a slow computation, or during some input/output (IO) operation, like a network access.

The UI frameworks that you might use from C# all operate using a single UI thread. This includes:

- WinForms
- WPF
- Silverlight

That UI thread is the only one that can control the contents of a particular window. It is also the only thread that checks for user actions and responds to them. If the thread is ever busy or blocked for more than a few tens of milliseconds, users will notice that the application feels sluggish.

Asynchronous code, even written manually, means that the UI thread can return to its primary job of checking the *message queue* for user events, and responding to them. It can also perform progress animations, and in recent versions of Windows, mouse hover animations, which are both important visual cues to users that give a good impression of the responsiveness of the application.

 The reason that all common UI frameworks use only one thread is to simplify synchronization. If there were many threads, one could try to read the width of a button, while another is in the process of laying out the controls. To avoid them conflicting, you'd need to use locking heavily, which would reduce the performance to the same as if there were only one thread.

An Analogy: The Cafe

I'd like to use an analogy to help with an intuitive grasp of the issues involved. If you feel you already understand, feel free to skip to the next section.

Imagine there's a small cafe, which sells customers toast for their breakfast. The only staff member is the owner. He is very concerned about customer service, but hasn't learned about asynchronous techniques.

The UI thread models the owner of the cafe very closely. In the same way that work inside a computer must be done by a thread, only cafe staff can do work at the cafe. In this case, there's only one staff member, just like there's only one UI thread.

The first customer asks the owner for a slice of toast. The owner gets the bread and starts the toaster. Then he watches the toaster while it cooks the toast. The customer asks where she can find some butter, but the owner ignores her, as he's blocked, watching the toaster. Five minutes later, the toast is done, and he brings it to the customer. By this time, a queue has built up, and the customer is annoyed about being ignored. Not ideal.

Now, lets see if we can teach the cafe owner how to be asynchronous.

First, he needs to make sure his toaster can operate asynchronously. When writing asynchronous code, we need to ensure that the long-running operation we are calling is able to call us back when it's done. In the same way, the toaster must have a timer, and must pop up the toast loudly when it's cooked, so he notices it.

The next thing is for him to ignore the toaster once he's started it. He should go back to serving the customers. In the same way, our asynchronous code must return once the long-running operation is started, so the UI thread can respond to user actions. There are two reasons for this:

- It feels more responsive to the user—the customer can ask for butter and isn't ignored
- The user can start another operation simultaneously—the next customer can also ask for their order to be started

The cafe owner can now process multiple customers at the same time, limited only by the number of toasters he has, and the time it takes him to fetch and carry the toast. But this comes with its own problems: he now finds it hard to remember which slices of toast are intended for which customers. In fact, the UI thread has no memory at all of which operations it's waiting for once it returns to processing user events.

So we need to attach a callback to the jobs as we start them, to remind us what to do when they are finished. For the cafe owner, this is as simple as writing the name of the customer on a label clipped to the toast. We may need something more complicated, and in general we'd like to be able to provide full instructions for what we need to do once the job is done.

With all of those things in place, the cafe owner is now fully asynchronous, and business booms. The customer experience is much better. There's less waiting, and the service feels much more responsive. I hope the analogy has helped with your intuition of why asynchrony is so important in UI applications.

Web Application Server Code

ASP.NET web servers don't have the same hard limit of one thread as UI code does. That said, there are still benefits to using asynchronous code. Long-running operations, especially remote database queries, are very common in web application code.

Depending on your version of IIS, there will be a limit on either the total number of threads used to process web requests, or the total number of concurrent requests being handled. If your requests spend most of their time waiting for a database query, it may seem a good idea to increase the number of simultaneous requests to increase the throughput your server can handle.

When a thread is blocked, waiting for something, it doesn't use any CPU time. However, don't assume that means it isn't using any of your server's resources. In fact, threads cause two significant overheads, even when they're blocked:

Memory
> Each managed thread reserves around a megabyte of virtual memory on Windows. This is no problem at all if you have a few tens of threads, but can easily get out of hand if you start using hundreds of threads. If the memory gets swapped out to disk, resuming the threads becomes slow.

Scheduler overhead
>   The operating system's scheduler is responsible for choosing which thread should be executed on which CPU, and when. Even when threads are blocked, the scheduler must consider them, to find whether they're become unblocked. This slows down context switches, and can slow the entire system.

Between them, these overheads can add to the load on your server, increasing latency and decreasing throughput.

Remember: the main characteristic of asynchronous code is that the thread that started a long-running operation is released to do other things. In the case of ASP.NET code, this thread is from the thread pool, so it is returned to the thread pool during the long-running operation. It can then process other requests, so fewer threads are needed to process the same number of requests.

Another Analogy: The Restaurant Kitchen

A web server is a close model of a restaurant. Many customers order food, and the kitchen tries to satisfy them as soon as it can.

Our kitchen has many chefs, with each chef representing a thread. They cook the dishes that the customers order, but at points during the preparation, each dish just needs to be in the oven for a while, and the chef has nothing to do. This mirrors the way that web requests usually need to make a database query that the web server has no part in.

In a blocking implementation of the kitchen, the chef will sit in front of the oven, waiting for the dish to be cooked. To model a thread exactly, these chefs have an odd contract where they aren't paid while they are waiting for food to cook, because a thread doesn't use CPU time when it is blocked. Maybe they read a newspaper.

But even if we don't have to pay them, and we can hire a new chef for every dish we need to cook, waiting chefs still take up space in the kitchen. We can't fit more than a few tens of chefs in the kitchen before it becomes hard to move around, and everyone's work slows down.

Of course, the asynchronous system works much better. Each time food is put in the oven, the chef notes down what dish it is, and what stage of preparation it's at, then finds a new task to do. When the time in the oven is done, any chef can pick the dish up and continue preparing it.

It's this efficient system that's so powerful in web servers. Only a few threads can manage a number of simultaneous requests that would have required hundreds before, or would have just been unfeasible because of the overheads. In fact, some web frameworks, notably *node.js*, reject the idea of multiple threads altogether, opting to use a single thread to process all the requests asynchronously. They can often handle more requests with one thread than a multithreaded, but blocking, system can handle in total. In the same way, one well-organized chef in an empty kitchen can cook more food than hundreds of chefs that spend all their time either tripping over each other or reading a newspaper.

Silverlight, Windows Phone, and Windows 8

The designers of Silverlight knew the benefits of asynchronous code in UI applications. So they decided to encourage everyone to write asynchronous code. They did this by removing most of the synchronous APIs from the framework. So, for example, web requests only exist as asynchronous calls.

Asynchronous code is contagious. If you call an asynchronous API, your code naturally ends up asynchronous as well. So in Silverlight, you *must* write asynchronous code—there is no option. There may be a `Wait` method, or some other way to consume an asynchronous API synchronously, by blocking while waiting to be called back. But if you do that, you lose all the advantages I've spoken about.

Silverlight for Windows Phone is, like its full name suggests, a type of Silverlight. Extra APIs are available, which wouldn't have been safe in Silverlight's in-browser environment, for example TCP sockets. Again though, only asynchronous versions of the APIs exist, encouraging you to write asynchronous code. If anything, it's more important to use asynchronous code on a mobile device, because resources are so scarce. Starting extra threads can have a serious effect on battery life.

Finally, despite not being technically related to Silverlight, Windows 8 applications take the same approach. There are a lot more APIs available, but only asynchronous versions of any APIs that might take longer than 50ms to complete are provided.

Parallel Code

Computers are being made with an increasing number of processor cores, all running independently of each other. Programs need to be able to take advantage of those cores, but any memory used by those programs can't be written from multiple cores at once, or the memory will be corrupted.

 Maybe we'll get better at using a *pure* (sometimes referred to as functional) style of programming, which doesn't manipulate state in memory, but deals with immutable values. That will help take advantage of parallelism, but is a bad fit for some programs. User interfaces need state. Databases *are* state.

The standard solution is to use mutual exclusion locks whenever multiple cores could potentially access the same memory. But this comes with its own problems. Your code will often take one lock, then make a method call or raise an event that takes another lock. Usually, it wasn't necessary to hold both locks at once, but the code was simpler.

This is false contention for the locks, and means that, overall, more threads end up waiting for locks when they could instead be doing useful work. In some situations, two threads both wait for a lock that the other holds, causing a deadlock. These bugs are hard to predict, hard to reproduce, and often hard to fix.

One of the most promising solutions is the *actors* model of computation. This is a design where each piece of writable memory can only exist inside one *actor*. The only way to use that memory is to send messages to that actor, which processes them, one at a time, and might reply with another message. This is exactly asynchronous programming. The operation of asking an actor for something is a typical asynchronous operation, because we can continue doing other things until the reply message arrives. And that means you can use async to do it, which we'll see in Chapter 10.

An Example

We'll look at an example of a desktop UI application that is badly in need of converting to an asynchronous style. The source is available online (*https://bitbucket.org/alexda vies74/faviconbrowser*). I recommend you follow along if you can, so get a copy (you can download it as a zip file if you don't use Mercurial) and open it in Visual Studio. Make sure to get the `default` branch, which is the synchronous version.

Run the program, and you'll see a window with a button. If you press the button, it will display the icons from some popular websites. It does this by downloading a file called `favicon.ico` that most websites contain (Figure 2-1).

Figure 2-1. Favicon browser running

Let's take a look at the code. The important part is the method that downloads the favicon and adds it to a WPF WrapPanel in the window.

```
private void AddAFavicon(string domain)
{
    WebClient webClient = new WebClient();
    byte[] bytes = webClient.DownloadData("http://" + domain + "/favicon.ico");
    Image imageControl = MakeImageControl(bytes);
    m_WrapPanel.Children.Add(imageControl);
}
```

You'll notice that this implementation is completely synchronous. The thread blocks while the icon is downloading. You'll probably also have noticed that the window becomes unresponsive for a few seconds when you press the button. As you know, that's because the UI thread is blocked while downloading all the icons, and can't return to process user events.

We'll use this example in the following chapters to walk through converting a synchronous program to an asynchronous one.

CHAPTER 3

Writing Asynchronous Code Manually

In this chapter, we'll talk about writing asynchronous code without the help of C# 5.0 and async. In a way, this is going over techniques you'll never have to use, but it's important to help understand what's really happening behind the scenes. Because of this, I'll go over the examples quickly, only drawing out the points that are helpful in understanding.

Some Asynchronous Patterns Used in .NET

As I mentioned before, Silverlight only provides asynchronous versions of APIs like web access. Here is an example of how you might download a web page and display it:

```
private void DumpWebPage(Uri uri)
{
    WebClient webClient = new WebClient();
    webClient.DownloadStringCompleted += OnDownloadStringCompleted;
    webClient.DownloadStringAsync(uri);
}

private void OnDownloadStringCompleted(object sender,
    DownloadStringCompletedEventArgs eventArgs)
{
    m_TextBlock.Text = eventArgs.Result;
}
```

This kind of API is called the *Event-based Asynchronous Pattern* (EAP). The idea is that instead of a single synchronous method to download the page, which blocks until it's done, one method and one event are used. The method looks just like the synchronous version, except it has a void return type. The event has a specially defined EventArgs type, which contains the value retrieved.

We sign up to the event immediately before calling the method. The method returns immediately, of course, because this is asynchronous code. Then, at some point in the future, the event will fire, and we can deal with it.

This pattern is obviously messy to use, not least because you have to split what would otherwise be a nice simple sequence of instructions into two methods. On top of that, the fact that you've signed up to an event adds a complication. If you go on to use the same instance of WebClient for another request, you might not expect that the original event will still be attached, and the handler will run again.

Another asynchronous pattern that features in .NET involves the IAsyncResult interface. One example is the method on Dns that looks up the IP address for a hostname, BeginGetHostAddresses. The design requires two methods, one called Begin*Method Name* which starts the operation, and one called End*MethodName* which you use in the callback to get the result.

```
private void LookupHostName()
{
    object unrelatedObject = "hello";
    Dns.BeginGetHostAddresses("oreilly.com", OnHostNameResolved, unrelatedObject);
}

private void OnHostNameResolved(IAsyncResult ar)
{
    object unrelatedObject = ar.AsyncState;
    IPAddress[] addresses = Dns.EndGetHostAddresses(ar);

    // Do something with addresses
    ...
}
```

At least this design doesn't suffer from the problems with leftover event handlers. However, it still adds extra complexity to the API, with two methods instead of one, and I find it unnatural.

Both of these patterns require you to split your procedure over two methods. The IAsyncResult pattern allows you to pass something from your first method into the second, as I have done with the string "hello". But the way it does it is messy, requiring you to pass something even if you didn't need to, and forcing you to cast it back from an object. The EAP also supports passing an object, in a similarly messy way.

Passing context between the methods is a general problem with asynchronous patterns. We'll see in the next section that a lambda is a solution, and you can use it in any of these situations.

The Simplest Asynchronous Pattern

Arguably the simplest code that has asynchronous behavior, without using async, involves passing a callback as a parameter to the method:

```
void GetHostAddress(string hostName, Action<IPAddress> callback)
```

I find this easier to use than the other patterns.

```
private void LookupHostName()
{
    GetHostAddress("oreilly.com", OnHostNameResolved);
}

private void OnHostNameResolved(IPAddress address)
{
    // Do something with address
    ...
}
```

Instead of using two methods, as I mentioned previously, you can use an anonymous method or lambda expression for the callback. This has the important benefit of allowing you to access variables from the first part of the method.

```
private void LookupHostName()
{
    int aUsefulVariable = 3;
    GetHostAddress("oreilly.com", address =>
        {
            // Do something with address and aUsefulVariable
            ...
        });
}
```

The lambda is a little hard to read, though, and often, if you are using multiple asynchronous APIs, you will need many lambdas nested within each other. Your code becomes deeply indented very quickly, and increasingly hard to work with.

The disadvantage of this simple approach is that any exceptions are no longer thrown to the caller. In the patterns used by .NET, the call to End*MethodName* or getting the Result property would rethrow the exception, so the originating code could deal with it. Instead, they could end up in the wrong place, or not handled at all.

An Introduction to Task

The Task Parallel Library was introduced in version 4.0 of the .NET Framework. Its most important class is Task, which represents an ongoing operation. A generic version, Task<T>, acts as a promise of a value (of type T) that will be available in the future, once the operation is done.

The async feature of C# 5.0 uses Task extensively, as we'll discuss later. However, even without async, you can use Task, and especially Task<T> to write asynchronous programs. To do this, you start the operation, which will return a Task<T>. Then use the ContinueWith method to register your callback.

```
private void LookupHostName()
{
    Task<IPAddress[]> ipAddressesPromise = Dns.GetHostAddressesAsync("oreilly.com");
    ipAddressesPromise.ContinueWith(_ =>
        {
            IPAddress[] ipAddresses = ipAddressesPromise.Result;


            // Do something with address
            ...
        });
}
```

The advantage of Task is that there is only one method required on Dns, making the API cleaner. All the logic related to the asynchronous behavior of the call can be inside the Task class, so that it need not be duplicated in every asynchronous method. This logic can do important things, like dealing with exceptions and SynchronizationContexts. These, as we'll discuss in Chapter 8, are useful for running the callback on a particular thread (for example, the UI thread).

On top of that, Task gives us the ability to work with asynchronous operations in an abstract way. We can use this composability to write utilities which work with Tasks to provide some behavior which is useful in a lot of situations. We'll see more about these utilities in Chapter 7.

The Problem with Manual Asynchrony

As we've seen, there are many ways to implement asynchronous programs. Some are neater than others. But hopefully you've seen they share one flaw. The procedure that you are intending to write has to be split into two methods: the actual method and the callback. Using an anonymous method or lambda for the callback mitigates some of this problem, but your code is left overly indented and hard to follow.

There's another problem here. We've spoken about methods that make one asynchronous call, but what happens if you need to make more than one? Even worse, what happens if you need to call asynchronous methods in a loop? Your only option is a recursive method, which is much harder to read than a normal loop.

```
private void LookupHostNames(string[] hostNames)
{
    LookUpHostNamesHelper(hostNames, 0);
}

private static void LookUpHostNamesHelper(string[] hostNames, int i)
{
    Task<IPAddress[]> ipAddressesPromise = Dns.GetHostAddressesAsync(hostNames[i]);
    ipAddressesPromise.ContinueWith(_ =>
        {
            IPAddress[] ipAddresses = ipAddressesPromise.Result;
```

```
        // Do something with address
        ...

        if (i + 1 < hostNames.Length)
        {
            LookUpHostNamesHelper(hostNames, i + 1);
        }
    });
}
```

Yuck.

One more problem caused by manual asynchronous programming in any of theses styles lies in consuming the asynchronous code that you've written. If you write some asynchronous, then want to use it from elsewhere in your program, you'll have to provide an asynchronous API to use. If consuming this kind of asynchronous API seemed difficult and messy, providing one is doubly so. And asynchronous code is contagious, so not only do you have to deal with asynchronous APIs, but so does your caller, and their caller, until the entire program is a mess.

Converting the Example to Use Manual Asynchronous Code

Recall that in "An Example" on page 10, we discussed a WPF UI app that was unresponsive because it downloaded icons from websites while blocking the UI thread. We'll now look at making it asynchronous using the manual techniques in this chapter.

The first task is to find an asynchronous version of the API I was using (WebClient.Down loadData). As we already saw, WebClient uses the Event-based Asynchronous Pattern (EAP), so we can sign up an event handler for the callback, then start the download.

```
private void AddAFavicon(string domain)
{
    WebClient webClient = new WebClient();
    webClient.DownloadDataCompleted += OnWebClientOnDownloadDataCompleted;
    webClient.DownloadDataAsync(new Uri("http://" + domain + "/favicon.ico"));
}

private void OnWebClientOnDownloadDataCompleted(object sender,
    DownloadDataCompletedEventArgs args)
{
    Image imageControl = MakeImageControl(args.Result);
    m_WrapPanel.Children.Add(imageControl);
}
```

Of course, our logic that really belongs together needs to be split into two methods. I prefer not to use a lambda with the EAP because the lambda would appear before the actual call to start the download, which I find unreadable.

This version of the example is also available online, under the branch `manual`. If you run it, not only does the UI remain responsive, but the icons appear gradually. Because of that, we've introduced a bug. Now, because all the download operations are started together (before any have finished) the icons are ordered by how quickly each downloaded, rather than by the order in which I requested them. If you'd like to check that you understand how to do manual asynchronous coding, I recommend fixing this bug. One solution is available under the branch `orderedManual`, and involves transforming the loop to a recursive method. More efficient solutions are also possible.

CHAPTER 4

Writing Async Methods

Now we know how great asynchronous code is, but how hard it is to write? It's time to look at the C# 5.0 async feature. As we saw previously in "What Async Does" on page 3, a method marked async is allowed to contain the await keyword.

```
private async void DumpWebPageAsync(string uri)
{
    WebClient webClient = new WebClient();
    string page = await webClient.DownloadStringTaskAsync(uri);
    Console.WriteLine(page);
}
```

The await expression in this example transforms the method, so it pauses during the download, then resumes when the download is done. This transformation makes the method asynchronous. In this chapter, we'll explore writing async methods like this one.

Converting the Favicon Example to Async

We'll now modify the favicon browser example from earlier to make use of async. If you can, open the original version of the example (the default branch) and try to convert it by adding async and await keywords before reading any further.

The important method is AddAFavicon, which downloads the icon, then adds it to the UI. We want to make this method asynchronous, so that the UI thread is free to respond to user actions during the download. The first step is to add the async keyword to the method. It appears in the method signature in the same way that the static keyword does.

Then, we need to wait for the download using the await keyword. In terms of C# syntax, await acts as a unary operator, like the ! not operator, or the (*type*) cast operator. It is placed to the left of an expression and means to wait for that expression asynchronously.

Finally, the call to `DownloadData` must be changed to instead call the asynchronous version, `DownloadDataTaskAsync`.

 An async method isn't automatically asynchronous. Async methods just make it easier to consume other asynchronous methods. They start running synchronously, until they call an asynchronous method and await it. When they do so, they necessarily become asynchronous themselves. Sometimes, an async method never awaits anything, in which case it runs synchronously.

```
private async void AddAFavicon(string domain)
{
    WebClient webClient = new WebClient();
    byte[] bytes = await webClient.DownloadDataTaskAsync("http://" + domain + "/
favicon.ico");
    Image imageControl = MakeImageControl(bytes);
    m_WrapPanel.Children.Add(imageControl);
}
```

Compare this to the other two versions of this code we've looked at. It *looks* much more like the original synchronous version of the code. There's no extra method, just a little extra code in the same structure. However, it *behaves* much more like the asynchronous version that we wrote in "Converting the Example to Use Manual Asynchronous Code" on page 17.

Task and await

Let's break down the `await` expression we've written. Here is the signature of the `WebClient.DownloadStringTaskAsync` method:

```
Task<string> DownloadStringTaskAsync(string address)
```

The return type is `Task<string>`. As I said in "An Introduction to Task" on page 15, a `Task` represents an ongoing operation, and its subclass `Task<T>` represents an operation that will have a result of type *T* at some point in the future. You can think of `Task<T>` as a promise of a *T* when the long-running operation completes.

`Task` and `Task<T>` can both represent asynchronous operations, and both have the ability to call back your code when the operation is done. To use that ability manually, you use their `ContinueWith` methods to pass a delegate containing the code to execute when the long-running operation is done. `await` uses the same ability to execute the rest of your async method in the same way.

If you apply `await` to a `Task<T>`, it becomes an *await expression*, and the whole expression has type *T*. That means you can assign the result of awaiting to a variable and use it in the rest of the method, as we've seen in the examples. However, when you await a non-generic `Task`, it becomes an *await statement*, and can't be assigned to anything, just like a call to a `void` method. This makes sense, as a `Task` doesn't promise a result value, it only represents the operation itself.

```
await smtpClient.SendMailAsync(mailMessage);
```

There is nothing stopping us from splitting up the `await` expression, so we can access the `Task` directly, or do something else, before awaiting it.

```
Task<string> myTask = webClient.DownloadStringTaskAsync(uri);
// Do something here
string page = await myTask;
```

It is important to fully understand the implications of this. The method `DownloadString` `TaskAsync` is executed on the first line. It begins executing synchronously, in the current thread, and once it has started the download, it returns a `Task<string>`, still in the current thread. It's only later when we await that `Task<string>` that the compiler does something special. This is all still true if you write the `await` on the same line as the call to the asynchronous method.

The long-running operation starts as soon as the call to `DownloadStringTaskAsync` is made, which gives us a very simple way to perform multiple asynchronous operations concurrently. We can just start multiple operations, keeping all the `Task`s, then await them all afterwards.

```
Task<string> firstTask = webClient1.DownloadStringTaskAsync("http://oreilly.com");
Task<string> secondTask = webClient2.DownloadStringTaskAsync("http://simple-
talk.com");
string firstPage = await firstTask;
string secondPage = await secondTask;
```

 This is a dangerous way to await multiple `Task`s, if they may throw exceptions. If both operations throw an exception, the first `await` will propagate its exception, which means `secondTask` is never awaited. Its exception will not be observed, and depending on .NET version and settings, may be lost or even rethrown on an unexpected thread, terminating the process. We'll see better ways to do this in Chapter 7.

Async Method Return Types

There are three return types that a method marked `async` may have:

- `void`
- `Task`
- `Task<T>` for some type *T*

No other return type is allowed because async methods in general aren't finished when they return. Typically, an async method will await a long-running operation, which means that the method returns quickly, but will resume in the future. That means no sensible result value is available when the method returns. The result will be available later.

 I'll make the distinction between the *return* type of a method—for example, `Task<string>`—and the *result* type that the programmer actually intends to give to the caller, which in this case is `string`. In normal non-async methods, the return type and the result type are always the same, but the difference is important for async methods.

It's obvious that `void` is a reasonable choice of return type in an asynchronous situation. A `async void` method is a "fire and forget" asynchronous operation. The caller can never wait for any result, and can't know when the operation completes or whether it was successful. You should use `void` when you know that no caller will ever need to know when the operation is finished or whether it succeeded. In practice, this means that `void` is used very rarely. The most common use of `async void` methods is in the boundary between async code and other code, for example a UI event handler must return `void`.

Async methods that return `Task` allow the caller to wait for the operation to finish, and propagate any exception that happened during the asynchronous operation. When no result value is needed, an `async Task` method is better than an `async void` method because it allows the caller to also use `await` to wait for it, making ordering and exception handling easier.

Finally, async methods that return `Task<T>`, for example `Task<string>`, are used when the asynchronous operation has a result value.

Async, Method Signatures, and Interfaces

The `async` keyword appears in the declaration of a method, just like the `public` or `static` keywords do. Despite that, `async` is *not* part of the signature of the method, in terms of overriding other methods, implementing interfaces, or being called.

The only effect that the `async` keyword has is on the compilation of the method to which it is applied, unlike the other keywords that are applied to a method, which change how it interacts with the outside world. Because of this, the rules around overriding methods and implementing interfaces completely ignore the `async` keyword.

```
class BaseClass
{
    public virtual async Task<int> AlexsMethod()
    {
        ...
    }
}
```

```
class SubClass : BaseClass
{
    // This overrides AlexsMethod above
    public override Task<int> AlexsMethod()
    {
        ...
    }
}
```

Interfaces can't use `async` in a method declaration, simply because there is no need. If an interface requires that a method returns `Task`, the implementation may choose to use `async`, but whether it does or not is a choice for the implementing method. The interface doesn't need to specify whether to use `async` or not.

The return Statement in Async Methods

The `return` statement has different behavior in an async method. Remember that in a normal non-async method, use of the `return` statement depends on the return type of the method:

`void` *methods*
> `return` statements must just be `return;`, and are optional

Methods that return a type T
> `return` must have an expression of type *T* (for example `return 5+x;`) and must exist at the end of the method on all code paths

In a method marked `async`, the rules apply in different situations:

`void` *methods and methods that return* `Task`
> `return` statements must just be `return;` and are optional

Methods that return `Task<T>`
> `return` must have an expression of type *T* and must exist at the end of the method on all code paths

In async methods, the return type of the method is different from the type of the expression found in the `return` statement. The compiler transformation can be thought to wrap up the value you return in a `Task<T>` before giving it to the caller. Of course, in reality, the `Task<T>` is created immediately, and only filled with your result value later, once any long-running operation is done.

Async Methods Are Contagious

As we've seen, the best way to consume a `Task` returned by an asynchronous API is to await it in an async method. When you do this, your method will typically return `Task` as well. To get the benefit of the asynchronous style, the code that calls your method must not block waiting for your `Task` to complete, and so your caller will probably also await you.

Here's an example of a helper method I've written that gets the number of characters on a web page, and returns them asynchronously.

```
private async Task<int> GetPageSizeAsync(string url)
{
    WebClient webClient = new WebClient();
    string page = await webClient.DownloadStringTaskAsync(url);
    return page.Length;
}
```

To use it, I need to write another async method, which returns its result asynchronously as well:

```
private async Task<string> FindLargestWebPage(string[] urls)
{
    string largest = null;
    int largestSize = 0;
    foreach (string url in urls)
    {
        int size = await GetPageSizeAsync(url);

        if (size > largestSize)
        {
            size = largestSize;
            largest = url;
        }
    }

    return largest;
}
```

In this way, we end up writing chains of async methods, each awaiting the next. Async is a contagious programming model, and it can easily pervade a whole codebase. But I think that because async methods are so easy to write, this isn't a problem at all.

Async Anonymous Delegates and Lambdas

Ordinary named methods can be async, and the two forms of anonymous methods can equally be async. The syntax is very much like normal methods. Here is how to make an asynchronous anonymous delegate:

```
Func<Task<int>> getNumberAsync = async delegate { return 3; };
```

And here is an async lambda:

```
Func<Task<string>> getWordAsync = async () => "hello";
```

All the same rules apply in these as in ordinary async methods. You can use them to keep code concise, and to capture closures, in exactly the same way you would in non-async code.

CHAPTER 5

What await Actually Does

There are two ways to think about the async feature of C# 5.0, and in particular what happens at an `await` keyword:

- As a language feature, which has a defined behavior that you can learn
- As a compile-time transformation, that is *syntactic sugar* for a more complex piece of C# that doesn't use async

Both are completely true; they are two sides of the same coin. In this chapter, we will concentrate on the first way of looking at async. In Chapter 14, we'll look at it from the other point of view, which is more complex but provides some details that will make debugging and performance considerations more clear.

Hibernating and Resuming a Method

When the execution of your program reaches an `await` keyword, we want two things to happen:

- The current thread executing your code should be released to make your code asynchronous. That means from a normal, synchronous, point of view, your method should return.
- When the `Task` that you awaited is complete, your method should continue from where it used to be, as if it hadn't returned earlier.

To achieve this behavior, your method must pause when it reaches an `await`, and then resume at a later point.

I think of this process as a small scale version of when you *hibernate* a computer (S4 sleep). The current state of the method is stored away, and the method exits completely. When a computer hibernates, the dynamic, running state of the computer is saved to disk, and it turns completely off. Just as you can unplug the power supply from a hibernated computer with no ill effects, an awaiting method uses no resources other than a little memory, as the thread that executed it has been released.

To take the analogy further, a blocking method is much more like when you *suspend* a computer (S3 sleep). It uses fewer resources, but fundamentally it's still running.

Ideally, the programmer shouldn't be able to detect that this hibernation has taken place. Despite the fact that hibernating and resuming a method mid-execution is a fairly complex operation, C# will make sure that your code is resumed as if it nothing had happened.

The State of the Method

Just to make it clear exactly how much work C# is doing for you when you use `await`, I'd like to think about all the details it needs to remember about the state of your method.

First, the values of all the local variables of your method are remembered. This includes the values of:

- The parameters of your method
- Any variables you've defined which are in scope
- Any other variables, for example loop counters
- The `this` variable, if your method is non-static. In that way, the member variables of your class are available when the method resumes.

All of these are stored in an object on the .NET garbage collected heap. So, when you use `await`, an object is allocated, which uses some resources, but won't cause a performance problem in most circumstances.

C# also remembers where in the method the `await` was reached. This can be stored using a number to represent which of the `await` keywords in the method we are at currently.

There's no restriction on how `await` expressions can be used. For example, they can be used as part of a larger expression, perhaps involving more than one `await`:

```
int myNum = await AlexsMethodAsync(await myTask, await StuffAsync());
```

This adds extra requirements to remember the state of the rest of the expression while awaiting something. In this example, the result of `await myTask` needs to be remembered while we run `await StuffAsync()`. .NET intermediate language (IL) stores this kind of sub-expression on a stack, so that stack is what the `await` keyword needs to store.

On top of this, when the program reaches the first `await` in a method, the method returns. Unless it is an `async void` method, a `Task` is returned at that point, so the caller can wait for us to complete somehow. C# must also store a way to manipulate that returned `Task`, so that when our method is done, the `Task` can become completed, and execution can move back up the asynchronous chain of methods. The exact mechanism for this is the subject of Chapter 14.

Context

As part of its effort to make the process of awaiting as transparent as possible, C# captures various kinds of context at an await, which are then restored when the method is resumed.

The most important of these is *synchronization context*, which can be used to resume the method on a particular type of thread, amongst other things. This is particularly important for UI applications, which can only manipulate their UI on the correct thread. Synchronization contexts are a complex topic, and Chapter 8 contains more details.

Other kinds of context are also captured from the calling thread. These are all controlled via a class of the same name, so I'll list some important types of context by their classes here:

ExecutionContext
> This is the parent context, all the other contexts are a part of it. It is the system that .NET features like Task use to capture and propagate context, but has no behavior of its own.

SecurityContext
> This is where we find any security information that would normally be confined to the current thread. If your code needs to run as a particular user, you may be *impersonating* that user, or ASP.NET may be doing impersonation for you. In that case, the impersonation is stored in the SecurityContext

CallContext
> This allows the programmer to store custom data that should be available for the lifetime of a logical thread. Although considered bad practice in a lot of situations, it can avoid excessive numbers of method parameters as various context is passed around the program. LogicalCallContext is a related system that works across AppDomains.

 It's worth noting that *thread local storage*, which is similar in purpose to CallContext, doesn't work in asynchronous situations, because the thread is released during the long-running operation, and may be used for other things. Your method could be resumed on a completely different thread.

C# will restore these types of context when your method is resumed. Restoring the context has some cost, so, for example, a program that makes heavy use of async could run a lot slower if it also uses impersonation. I advise avoiding .NET features that create context unless you know it is really necessary.

Where await Can't Be Used

await can be used in any method marked async, at most places in the method. But there are a few places where you can't use await. I'll explain why it wouldn't make sense to allow await in these situations.

catch and finally Blocks

While is perfectly allowed to use await in a try block, it is not valid C# to use it inside a catch or finally block. Often in catch blocks, and always in finally blocks, the exception is still in the process of unwinding the stack, and will be rethrown later in the block. If an await were used before that point, the stack would be different, and the behavior of the rethrow would be very hard to define.

Remember that instead of using await in a catch block, it is always possible to use it after the catch block, by using either a return statement or a bool variable to remember whether the original operation threw an exception. For example, if you wanted to write this invalid C#:

```
try
{
    page = await webClient.DownloadStringTaskAsync("http://oreilly.com");
}
catch (WebException)
{
    page = await webClient.DownloadStringTaskAsync("http://oreillymirror.com");
}
```

You could instead write this:

```
bool failed = false;
try
{
    page = await webClient.DownloadStringTaskAsync("http://oreilly.com");
}
catch (WebException)
{
    failed = true;
}

if (failed)
{
    page = await webClient.DownloadStringTaskAsync("http://oreillymirror.com");
}
```

lock Blocks

A lock is a way for the programmer to prevent other threads accessing the same objects as the current thread at the same time. Because asynchronous code generally releases the thread it started on, and may be called back an indeterminate amount of time later on a thread which may be different to the original, it makes no sense to hold a lock across an await.

In some situations, it's important to protect your object from concurrent access, but it isn't important that no other thread accesses the object during an await. In those situations, you have the option of writing the slightly verbose code that explicitly locks twice:

```
lock (sync)
{
    // Prepare for async operation
}

int myNum = await AlexsMethodAsync();

lock (sync)
{
    // Use result of async operation
}
```

Alternatively, you could use a library that handles concurrency control for you—for example, NAct, which is introduced in Chapter 10.

If you're unlucky, you may need to hold some kind of lock over the execution of an asynchronous operation. When this happens, you need to think hard, because in general it's very difficult to lock resources across an asynchronous call without inviting serious contention issues and deadlocks. It may be best to redesign your program.

LINQ Query Expressions

C# has syntax to make it easier to write declarative queries for filtering, transforming, ordering, and grouping data. Those queries can then be executed on .NET collections, or translated for execution on databases or other data sources.

```
IEnumerable<int> transformed = from x in alexsInts
                               where x != 9
                               select x + 2;
```

It is not valid C# to use await in most places in a Query Expression. This is because those places are transformed by the compiler to lambda expressions, and as such, the lambda expression would need to be marked async. The syntax to mark these implicit lambda expressions async simply doesn't exist, and would probably be really confusing if it did.

You can always write the equivalent expression using the extension methods that LINQ uses internally. Then the lambda expressions become explicit, and you can mark them as async to use await.

```
IEnumerable<Task<int>> tasks = alexsInts
    .Where(x => x != 9)
    .Select(async x => await DoSomthingAsync(x) + await DoSomthingElseAsync(x));

IEnumerable<int> transformed = await Task.WhenAll(tasks);
```

To gather the results, I've used Task.WhenAll, which is a utility for working with collections of Tasks that we'll look at in detail in Chapter 7.

Unsafe Code

Code that is marked unsafe may not contain await. Unsafe code should be very rare and should be kept to self-contained methods that don't need to be asynchronous. The await compiler transformation would break the unsafe code in most situations, anyway.

Exception Capture

Exceptions in async methods are designed to act very similarly to exceptions in normal synchronous methods. However, the extra complexity of async means that there are subtle differences. Here, I'll talk about how async makes exception handling simple, and I'll describe the caveats in more detail in Chapter 9.

When it completes, the Task type has a concept of whether it finished successfully or failed. This is most simply exposed by the IsFaulted property, which is true when an exception is thrown during the execution of the Task. The await keyword is aware of this and will rethrow the exception contained in the Task.

 If you're familiar with the .NET exception system, you may be wondering whether the stack trace of the exception is preserved correctly when the exception is rethrown. That has always been impossible in the past; each exception could only be thrown once. However, in .NET 4.5 that limitation was fixed, with a new class called ExceptionDispatch Info, which cooperates with Exception to capture and rethrow an exception with the correct stack trace.

The async method is also aware of exceptions. Any exception that happens during an async method, and isn't caught, is placed into the Task returned to the caller. When that happens, if the caller is already awaiting the Task, the exception will be thrown there. In this way, the exception propagates back through the callers, forming a virtual stack trace in exactly the same way it would in synchronous code.

I call this a *virtual* stack trace, because the stack is a concept that a single thread has, and in async code, the actual stack of the current thread may be very different from the stack trace that an exception produces. The exception captures the stack trace of the programmer's *intention*, with the methods that the programmer called, rather than the details of how C# chose to execute parts of those methods.

Async Methods Are Synchronous Until Needed

I said before that async methods are only asynchronous if they consume an asynchronous method with an `await`. Until that happens, they run in the thread that called them, just the same as a normal synchronous method. This sometimes has very real implications, especially when it's possible for an entire chain of async methods to complete synchronously.

Remember that the async method only pauses when it reaches the first `await`. Even then, it sometimes doesn't need to, because sometimes the `Task` given to an `await` is already complete. A `Task` can be already complete in these situations:

- It was created complete, by the `Task.FromResult` utility method, which we'll explore further in Chapter 7
- It was returned by an async method that never reached an `await`
- It ran a genuine asynchronous operation, but has now finished (perhaps because the current thread did something else before awaiting)
- It was returned by an async method that reached an `await`, but the `Task` it awaited was also already complete

Because of the last possibility, something interesting happens when you await a `Task` that's already complete, deep in a chain of async methods. The entire chain is likely to complete synchronously. That's because in a chain of async methods, the first `await` to be called is always the deepest one. The others are only reached after the deepest method has had a chance to return synchronously.

You might wonder why you would use async in the first place if the first or second possibilities happened. If those methods were guaranteed to always return synchronously, you'd be right, and it would be more efficient to write synchronous code than to write async methods with no `await`. However, there are situations where methods would *sometimes* return synchronously. For example, a method that cached its results in memory could return synchronously when the result is available from the cache, but asynchronously when it needs to make a network request. You may also want to make methods return `Task` or `Task<T>` to future-proof a codebase, when you know there's a good chance you'd like to make those methods asynchronous at some point down the line.

CHAPTER 6

The Task-Based Asynchronous Pattern

The Task-based Asynchronous Pattern (TAP) is a set of recommendations from Microsoft for writing asynchronous APIs in .NET using `Task`. The document (*http://www.microsoft.com/en-gb/download/details.aspx?id=19957*) by Stephen Toub from the parallel programming team at Microsoft has good examples and is worth a read.

The pattern makes APIs that can be consumed using `await`, and while using `async` produces methods that follow the pattern, it's often useful to use `Task` manually. In this chapter, I'll explain the pattern, and techniques to work with it.

What the TAP Specifies

I'll assume we already know how to design a good method signature for synchronous C# code:

- It should have a few parameters, or maybe none. `ref` and `out` parameters should be avoided if possible.
- It should have a return type, if it makes sense, which really expresses the result of the code inside the method, as opposed to a success indicator like in some C++ code.
- It should have a name that explains the behavior of the method, without extra notation.
- Common or expected failures should be part of the return type, while unexpected failures should throw exceptions.

Here is a well designed synchronous method, which is part of the `Dns` class:

```
public static IPHostEntry GetHostEntry(string hostNameOrAddress)
```

The TAP gives the same level of guidelines on designing an asynchronous method, based on your existing skills with synchronous methods. Here they are:

- It should have the same parameters as an equivalent synchronous method would. `ref` and `out` parameters must never be used.

- It should return `Task`, or `Task<T>`, depending on whether the synchronous method would have a return type. That task should complete at some point in the future, providing the result value the method.

- It should be named *Name*Async, where *Name* is the name the equivalent synchronous method would have had.

- An exception caused by a mistake in the usage of the method may be thrown directly from the method. Any other exception should be placed in the `Task`.

And here is a well-designed TAP method:

```
public static Task<IPHostEntry> GetHostEntryAsync(string hostNameOrAddress)
```

This may all seem completely obvious, but as we saw in "Some Asynchronous Patterns Used in .NET" on page 13, this is the third formal asynchronous pattern that has been used in the .NET framework, and I'm sure others have used countless informal ways to write asynchronous code.

The key idea of the TAP is for the asynchronous method to return a `Task`, which encapsulates the promise of a long-running operation completing in the future. Without that idea, previous asynchronous patterns needed to either add extra parameters to the method, or add extra methods or events to the interface to support the callback mechanism. `Task` can contain whatever infrastructure is needed to support the callback, without polluting your code with the details.

An added benefit is that, because the mechanics of the asynchronous callback are now in `Task`, they don't need to be duplicated everywhere an asynchronous call is made. In turn, that means the mechanics can afford to be more complicated and powerful, making it feasible to do things like restore context, including synchronization context, as the callback is made. It also provides a common API for dealing with asynchronous operations, making compiler features like async reasonable, which wouldn't have been reasonable with the other patterns.

Using Task for Compute-Intensive Operations

Sometimes, a long-running operation doesn't make any network requests or access the disk; it just takes a long time because it's a difficult calculation that needs a lot of processor time to complete. Of course, we can't expect to be able to do this without tying up a thread, like we could with a network access. But in programs with a user interface, we still want to avoid freezing the UI. To fix that, we have to return the UI thread to process other events and use a different thread for our long-running computation.

`Task` provides an easy way to do this, and you can use `await` with it like any other `Task` to update the UI when the computation is complete:

```
Task t = Task.Run(() => MyLongComputation(a, b));
```

`Task.Run` uses a thread from the `ThreadPool` to execute the delegate you give it. In this case, I've used a lambda to make it easy to pass my local variables to the computation. The resulting `Task` is started immediately, and we can await it just like any other `Task`:

```
await Task.Run(() => MyLongComputation(a, b));
```

This is a very simple way do work on a background thread.

For example, if you need more control over which thread does the computation or how it is queued, `Task` has a static property called `Factory` of type `TaskFactory`. This has a method `StartNew` with various overloads for controlling the execution of your computation:

```
Task t = Task.Factory.StartNew(() => MyLongComputation(a, b),
                               cancellationToken,
                               TaskCreationOptions.LongRunning,
                               taskScheduler);
```

If you're writing a library that contains a lot of compute-intensive methods, you may be tempted to provide asynchronous versions of your methods that call `Task.Run` to start the work in a background thread. That's not a good idea, because the caller of your API knows more about the threading requirements of the application than you do. For example, in web applications, there is no benefit to using the thread pool; the only thing that should be optimized is the total number of threads. `Task.Run` is a very easy call to make, so leave your callers to do it if they need to.

Creating a Puppet Task

The TAP is really easy to consume, so you'll naturally want to provide it in all the APIs you make. We already know how to do this when you're consuming other TAP APIs, using an async method. But what about when the long-running operation isn't already available as a TAP API? Maybe it's an API using another asynchronous pattern. Maybe you're not consuming an API, but you're doing something asynchronous completely manually.

The tool to use here is `TaskCompletionSource<T>`. It is a way to create a `Task` which is your puppet. You can make the `Task` complete at any point you like, and you can make it fault by giving it an exception at any point you like.

Let's look at an example. Suppose you'd like to encapsulate a prompt displayed to the user with this method:

```
Task<bool> GetUserPermission()
```

The prompt is a custom dialog you've written that asks the user for consent of some kind. Because the permission could be needed at many points in your application, it's important to make it one easy method to call. This is a perfect place to use an asynchronous method, because you want to release the UI thread to actually display the dialog. But, it isn't even close to the traditional asynchronous method that calls through to a network request or other long-running operation. Here, we're awaiting the user. Let's look at the body of the method.

```
private Task<bool> GetUserPermission()
{
    // Make a TaskCompletionSource so we can return a puppet Task
    TaskCompletionSource<bool> tcs = new TaskCompletionSource<bool>();

    // Create the dialog ready
    PermissionDialog dialog = new PermissionDialog();

    // When the user is finished with the dialog, complete the Task using SetResult
    dialog.Closed += delegate { tcs.SetResult(dialog.PermissionGranted); };

    // Show the dialog
    dialog.Show();

    // Return the puppet Task, which isn't completed yet
    return tcs.Task;
}
```

Notice that the method isn't marked async; we're creating a Task manually, so we don't want the compiler to generate one for us. The TaskCompletionSource<bool> creates the Task, and makes it available as a property for us to return. We can later use the SetResult method on the TaskCompletionSource to make the Task complete.

Because we've followed the TAP, our caller can just await the user's permission. The call is very neat.

```
if (await GetUserPermission())
{ ....
```

One annoyance is there isn't a non-generic version of TaskCompletionSource<T>. However, because Task<T> is a subclass of Task, you can use a Task<T> anywhere you wanted a Task. In turn that means you can use a TaskCompletionSource<T>, and the Task<T> returned by the Task property is a perfectly valid Task. I tend to use a TaskCompletionSource<object> and call SetResult(null) to complete it. You could easily create a non-generic TaskCompletionSource if you wanted, based on the generic one.

Interacting with Old Asynchronous Patterns

The .NET team have created TAP versions of all the important asynchronous APIs in the framework. But it is interesting to know how to build a TAP method from non-TAP asynchronous code, in case you need to interact with some existing asynchronous codebase. It's also an interesting example of how to use TaskCompletionSource<T>.

Let's examine the DNS lookup example that I used earlier. In .NET 4.0, the asynchronous version of the DNS lookup method used the IAsyncResult asynchronous pattern. That means it consisted of a Begin method and an End method:

```
IAsyncResult BeginGetHostEntry(string hostNameOrAddress,
                               AsyncCallback requestCallback,
                               object stateObject)

IPHostEntry EndGetHostEntry(IAsyncResult asyncResult)
```

Typically, you would consume this API using a lambda as the callback and call the End method from inside the lambda. That's exactly what we'll do here, but instead of actually doing anything in the callback, we'll just use a TaskCompletionSource<T> to complete a Task.

```
public static Task<IPHostEntry> GetHostEntryAsync(string hostNameOrAddress)
{
    TaskCompletionSource<IPHostEntry> tcs = new TaskCompletionSource<IPHostEntry>();
    Dns.BeginGetHostEntry(hostNameOrAddress, asyncResult =>
        {
            try
            {
                IPHostEntry result = Dns.EndGetHostEntry(asyncResult);
                tcs.SetResult(result);
            }
            catch (Exception e)
            {
                tcs.SetException(e);
            }
        }, null);

    return tcs.Task;
}
```

This code is made more complex by the possibility of an exception. If the DNS resolve fails, an exception will be thrown when we call EndGetHostEntry. That's why the IAsyncResult pattern uses a convoluted system with an End method, rather than just passing the result into the callback directly. When an exception is thrown, we should put it into our TaskCompletionSource<T> so our caller can get the exception according to the TAP style.

In fact, there were enough asynchronous APIs following this pattern that the .NET framework team made a utility method to turn them into a TAP version, which is available to us as well:

```
Task t = Task<IPHostEntry>.Factory.FromAsync<string>(Dns.BeginGetHostEntry,
                                                      Dns.EndGetHostEntry,
                                                      hostNameOrAddress,
                                                      null);
```

It takes the Begin and End methods as delegates, and uses a mechanism very similar to the way we did it before. It probably does it more efficiently than our simple approach though.

Cold and Hot Tasks

When the Task Parallel Library originally introduced the `Task` type in .NET 4.0, it had the concept of a *cold* `Task`, which still needs to be started, as opposed to a *hot* `Task`, which is already running. So far, we've only dealt with hot `Tasks`.

The TAP specifies that all `Tasks` must be hot before they are returned from a method. Luckily, all the techniques we've spoken about for creating a `Task` create a hot one. The exception is the `TaskCompletionSource<T>` technique, which doesn't really have the concept of a hot or cold task. You just need to make sure to complete the `Task` at some point yourself.

Up-Front Work

We already know that when you call a TAP asynchronous method, the method runs on the current thread, as with any other method. The difference is that a TAP method will probably not have actually finished working before it returns. It will return a `Task` quickly, and that `Task` will complete when the actual work is done.

Having said that, some code in the method will run synchronously, in the current thread. In the case of an async method, that will be at least the code up to, and including the operand of, the first `await`, as we saw in "Async Methods Are Synchronous Until Needed" on page 31.

The TAP recommends that the synchronous work done by a TAP method should be the minimum amount possible. You can check that the arguments are valid and scan a cache to avoid the long-running operation, but you shouldn't do a slow computation. Hybrid methods, which do some computation, followed by a network access or something similar are good, but you should use `Task.Run` to move the computation to a background thread. Imagine the routine that uploads an image to a website, but needs to resize it first to save bandwidth:

```
Image resized = await Task.Run(() => ResizeImage(originalImage));
await UploadImage(resized);
```

While this is important in a UI application, it has no practical benefits in a web application. Nevertheless, when we see a method that appears to follow the TAP, we expect it to return quickly. Anyone that takes your code and moves it to a UI application will be in for a surprise if you did a slow picture resize synchronously.

CHAPTER 7

Utilities for Async Code

The Task-based Asynchronous Pattern is designed to make it easy to create utilities for working with Tasks. Because all TAP methods give you a Task, any special behavior we write for one TAP method, we can reuse against others. In this chapter, we'll look at some utilities for working with Task, including:

- Methods that look like TAP methods, but have useful special behavior rather than being asynchronous calls themselves

- Combinators, which are methods which process Tasks, generating useful new Tasks based on them

- Tools for canceling and showing progress during asynchronous operations

While a lot of these utilities already exist, it's useful to see how easy it is to implement them yourself, in case you need similar tools in the future that aren't provided by the .NET Framework.

Delaying for a Period of Time

The most simple long-running operation that you might want to perform is possibly to do absolutely nothing for a length of time. This is the equivalent of Thread.Sleep in the synchronous world. In fact, you could implement it using Thread.Sleep in conjunction with Task.Run:

```
await Task.Run(() => Thread.Sleep(100));
```

But this simple approach is wasteful. A thread is being used solely to block for the time period, which is a waste. There is already a way to have .NET call your code back after a period of time without using any threads, the System.Threading.Timer class. A more efficient approach would be to set up a Timer, then use a TaskCompletionSource to create a Task that we can cause to complete when the Timer fires:

```
private static Task Delay(int millis)
{
    TaskCompletionSource<object> tcs = new TaskCompletionSource<object>();
    Timer timer = new Timer(_ => tcs.SetResult(null), null, millis, Timeout.Infinite);
    tcs.Task.ContinueWith(delegate { timer.Dispose(); });
    return tcs.Task;
}
```

Of course, this is such a useful little tool that it's provided in the framework. It's called `Task.Delay`, and of course the framework version is more powerful, robust, and probably more efficient than mine.

Waiting for a Collection of Tasks

As we saw back in "Task and await" on page 20, it's very easy to run multiple asynchronous operations in parallel by calling them in turn, then awaiting them in turn. What we'll find out in Chapter 9 is that it's important that we await each and every `Task` that we start, otherwise exceptions can get lost.

The solution to this problem is to use `Task.WhenAll`, which is a utility that can take many `Task`s and produce one aggregated `Task` that will complete once all the inputs complete. Here is the simplest version of `WhenAll`, it has overloads for generic `Task<T>`s as well:

```
Task WhenAll(IEnumerable<Task> tasks)
```

The key difference between using `WhenAll` and just awaiting multiple tasks yourself is that `WhenAll` gets the behavior right when exceptions are thrown. You should always use `WhenAll` for this reason.

The generic version of `WhenAll` gives you an array containing the results of the individual `Task`s you gave it. That's for convenience rather than being necessary, because you still have access to the original `Task`s, so you can use their `Result` property, knowing that they must already be complete.

Let's revisit the favicon browser as an example. Remember that we now have a version that calls an `async void` method to begin downloading each icon in turn. That method then adds the icon to the window when the download is done. This approach is very efficient, as all the downloads happen in parallel, but there are two problems:

- The icons appear in the window in whichever order they finish downloading
- Because each icon is downloaded in its own `async void` method, any exceptions that escape it are rethrown in the UI thread, and dealing with them neatly would be hard

So let's refactor so that the method that loops through all the icons is itself async. That means we can take control of the asynchronous operations as a group. We'll start at the point after that refactor with this version that does each icon in turn:

```
private async void GetButton_OnClick(object sender, RoutedEventArgs e)
{
    foreach (string domain in s_Domains)
    {
        Image image = await GetFavicon(domain);
        AddAFavicon(image);
    }
}
```

Now we'll fix this so it does all the downloads in parallel, but still displays the icons in order. We first start all the downloads by calling GetFavicon and storing the Tasks in a List.

```
List<Task<Image>> tasks = new List<Task<Image>>();
foreach (string domain in s_Domains)
{
    tasks.Add(GetFavicon(domain));
}
```

Or, even better, if you like LINQ:

```
IEnumerable<Task<Image>> tasks = s_Domains.Select(GetFavicon);

// The IEnumerable from Select is lazy, so evaluate it to start the tasks
tasks = tasks.ToList();
```

Once we have the group of tasks, we give them to Task.WhenAll and it gives us a Task that will complete when all of the downloads are done, with all the results.

```
Task<Image[]> allTask = Task.WhenAll(tasks);
```

Then, all we have left to do is await the allTask, and use its results:

```
Image[] images = await allTask;
foreach (Image eachImage in images)
{
    AddAFavicon(eachImage);
}
```

So, we've successfully written something that's really quite a complex piece of parallel logic in only a few lines. The final result is available under the branch whenAll.

Waiting for Any One Task from a Collection

The other common tool you might need for working with multiple Tasks is to wait for the first to finish. This could be because you are requesting a resource from a variety of sources, and whichever response comes earliest can be used.

The tool for this job is Task.WhenAny. Here is a generic version. Again, there are lots of overloads, but this one is interesting.

```
Task<Task<T>> WhenAny(IEnumerable<Task<T>> tasks)
```

The signature of WhenAny is a little harder to understand than WhenAll, and this is for good reason. When exceptions are possible, WhenAny is a tool that needs to be used carefully. If you want to find out about all exceptions that happen in your program, you need to make sure that every single Task you make is awaited, or exceptions can get lost. Using WhenAny and simply forgetting about the other Tasks is equivalent to catching all exceptions and ignoring them, which is bad practice and tends to show up later as subtle bugs and invalid states.

The return type of WhenAny is Task<Task<T>>. That means after you've awaited it, you get a Task<T>. This Task<T> is whichever of the original ones completed first, and thus is always already completed when you get it. The reason that you are given the Task rather than just the T result is so you know which of the original Tasks finished first, so you can cancel and await all the others.

```
Task<Task<Image>> anyTask = Task.WhenAny(tasks);
Task<Image> winner = await anyTask;
Image image = await winner; // This always completes synchronously

AddAFavicon(image);

foreach (Task<Image> eachTask in tasks)
{
    if (eachTask != winner)
    {
        await eachTask;
    }
}
```

There's no harm in using the winner to update the UI as soon as it completes, but after that's done, you should await all the other Tasks as I have done here. Hopefully they will have all succeeded, and this extra code will have no effect on your program. But if one of them fails, this means you'll find out about it, and can fix the bug.

Creating Your Own Combinators

We call WhenAll and WhenAny asynchronous combinators. While they return Tasks, they aren't themselves asynchronous methods, but rather combine other Tasks in useful ways. You can also write your own combinators if you need them, so you have a palette of reusable parallel behaviors you can apply where you like.

Let's write a combinator as an example. Perhaps we'd like to add a timeout to any Task. Although we could write that from scratch fairly easily, it serves as a good example to make use of both Delay and WhenAny. In general, combinators are often easiest to implement using async, as in this case, but sometimes you won't need to.

```
private static async Task<T> WithTimeout<T>(Task<T> task, int time)
{
    Task delayTask = Task.Delay(time);
    Task firstToFinish = await Task.WhenAny(task, delayTask);

    if (firstToFinish == delayTask)
    {
```

```
    // The delay finished first - deal with any exception
    task.ContinueWith(HandleException);
    throw new TimeoutException();
}

    return await task; // If we reach here, the original task already finished
}
```

My technique is to create a `Task` using `Delay` that will complete after the timeout. I then use `WhenAny` on both that and the original `Task` so I resume at whichever is earlier, the operation finishing, or the timeout expiring. After that, it's a case of finding which has happened and either throwing a `TimeoutException` or returning the result.

Notice that I've been careful about exceptions in the case that the timeout expires. I've attached a continuation to the original `Task` using `ContinueWith`, which handles an exception if there is one. I know that the delay can never throw an exception, so I don't need to deal with it. The implementation of the `HandleException` method looks something like this:

```
    private static void HandleException<T>(Task<T> task)
    {
        if (task.Exception != null)
        {
            logging.LogException(task.Exception);
        }
    }
```

Obviously, exactly what to do here depends on your strategy for handling exceptions. By attaching this using `ContinueWith`, I've made sure that whenever the original `Task` does finish, however far in the future that may be, the code to check for an exception is run. Importantly, this doesn't hold up the main execution of the program, which already did whatever it needed to do when the timeout expired.

Cancelling Asynchronous Operations

Rather than being tied in to the `Task` type, cancellation in the TAP is enabled by the `CancellationToken` type. By convention, any TAP method which supports being canceled should have an overload that takes a `CancellationToken` after the normal parameters. An example in the framework is the `DbCommand` type, and its asynchronous methods that query a database. The simplest overload of `ExecuteNonQueryAsync` has no parameters.

```
    Task<int> ExecuteNonQueryAsync(CancellationToken cancellationToken)
```

We'll start by looking at how to cancel an asynchronous method we've called. To do that, we need `CancellationTokenSource`, which is a utility for creating `Cancellation` `Tokens` and also controlling them, in a similar way to how a `TaskCompletionSource` creates and controls a `Task`. The following code is incomplete, but shows the kind of technique you need:

```
CancellationTokenSource cts = new CancellationTokenSource();
cancelButton.Click += delegate { cts.Cancel(); };
int result = await dbCommand.ExecuteNonQueryAsync(cts.Token);
```

When you call `Cancel` on the `CancellationTokenSource`, the `CancellationToken` moves to a canceled state. It's possible to register a delegate to be called when that happens, but in practice, a much simpler polling approach to detecting whether your caller wants to cancel you is more effective. If you're writing a loop in an asynchronous method, and a `CancellationToken` is available, you should just call `ThrowIfCancellationRequested` in each iteration of the loop.

```
foreach (var x in thingsToProcess)
{
    cancellationToken.ThrowIfCancellationRequested();
    // Process x ...
}
```

When you call `ThrowIfCancellationRequested` on a `CancellationToken` which is canceled, it will throw an `OperationCanceledException`. The Task Parallel Library knows that this type of exception represents cancellation rather than a failure, and will treat it differently. For example, `Task` has a property called `IsCanceled` that automatically becomes true when an `OperationCanceledException` is thrown while executing an async method.

One neat feature of the token approach to cancellation is that the same `CancellationToken` can be distributed to as many parts of the asynchronous operation as you need, simply by passing it to them. Whether those parts run in parallel or sequentially, and whether they are computations involving loops or remote operations, the same token can cancel them all.

Returning Progress During an Asynchronous Operation

Aside from keeping the UI responsive, and giving the user the opportunity to cancel, another good way to improve the experience during an unavoidably slow operation is to indicate how much longer the user will have to wait. To do this, another pair of types for indicating progress are provided and recommended as part of the TAP. This time, you pass asynchronous methods an interface, `IProgress<T>`, which they can call to give an indication of how they're doing.

The `IProgress<T>` parameter is, by convention, placed right at the end of the parameters to the method, after any `CancellationToken`. Here is how you would add progress reporting to `DownloadDataTaskAsync`.

```
Task<byte[]> DownloadDataTaskAsync(Uri address,
                         CancellationToken cancellationToken,
                         IProgress<DownloadProgressChangedEventArgs> progress)
```

To use a method like this, you need to create an implementation of `IProgress<T>`. Luckily, one is provided that does exactly what is needed in most situations,

Progress<T>. You construct one of these, either passing a lambda into its constructor, or signing up to an event, to get notifications of new progress figures, which you can use to update your UI.

```
new Progress<int>(percentage => progressBar.Value = percentage);
```

The clever feature of Progress<T> is that it will capture the SynchronizationContext on construction, and use it to call your progress update code in the right thread. This is much the same as the behavior of the Task itself continuing after an await, so you don't need to worry about the fact that your IProgress<T> could be called from any thread.

If you'd like to report progress when writing a TAP method, you just need to call the Report method on the IProgress<T>.

```
progress.Report(percent);
```

The difficult part is to choose the type parameter T. This is the type of the object that you pass to Report, which is the same object that the caller's lambda is given. An int is a good choice for simple percentages, as I've used here, but sometimes you need more details. Be careful though, because that object will usually be consumed on a different thread to the one that made it. Use an immutable type to avoid problems.

CHAPTER 8

Which Thread Runs My Code?

As I've said before, asynchronous programming is all about threads. In C#, that means we need to understand which .NET thread is running our code at what points in the program, and what happens to the threads while long-running operations take place.

Before the First await

In each async method you write, some code will be before the first occurrence of the await keyword. Equally, some code is in the expression that gets awaited.

This code always runs in the calling thread. Nothing interesting happens before the first await.

 This is one of the most common misconceptions about async. Async never schedules your method to run on a background thread. The only way to do that is using something like Task.Run, which is explicitly for that purpose.

In the case of a UI application, that means the code before the first await runs in the UI thread. Likewise, in an ASP.NET web application, it runs in an ASP.NET worker thread.

Typically, you might run another async method as the expression being awaited on the line containing the first await. Because this expression is executed before the first await, it must also get run in the calling thread. That means the calling thread will continue executing code deep into your application, all the way until some method actually returns a Task. The method that does that might be a framework method, or it might be a method using TaskCompletionSource to construct a puppet Task. That method is the source of the asynchrony in your program—all the async methods are just propagating the asynchrony.

The code that's run before that first real asynchronous point is reached could be quite extensive, and in a UI application that code is all run by the UI thread, while the UI remains unresponsive. Hopefully, the code doesn't take too long, but it's important to remember that just using async won't guarantee your UI is responsive. If it does feel slow, get a performance profiler, and find out where the time is spent.

During the Asynchronous Operation

Which thread actually does the asynchronous operation?

That's a trick question. This is asynchronous code. For typical operations like network requests, there are no threads at all that are blocked waiting for the operation to complete.

 Of course, if you're using async to wait for a computation, for example using `Task.Run`, the thread pool thread performing the computation exists and is busy.

There is a thread waiting for network requests to complete, but it is shared between all network requests. It's called the *IO completion port* thread on Windows. When the network request completes, an interrupt handler in the operating system adds a job to a queue for the IO completion port. To perform 1000 network requests, the requests are all started, and as the responses arrive, they are processed in turn by the single IO completion port.

 In reality, there are usually a handful of IO completion port threads, to take advantage of multiple CPU cores. However, the number of threads is the same whether there are currently 10 outstanding network requests or 1000.

SynchronizationContext in Detail

SynchronizationContext is a class provided by the .NET Framework, which has the ability to run code in a particular type of thread. There are various Synchronization Contexts used by .NET, the most important of which are the UI thread contexts used by WinForms and WPF.

Instances of SynchronizationContext itself don't do anything very useful, so all actual instances of it tend to be subclasses. It also has static members which let you read and control the *current* SynchronizationContext. The current SynchronizationContext is a property of the current thread. The idea is that at any point that you're running in a special thread, you should be able to get the current SynchronizationContext and store it. Later, you can use it to run code back on the special thread you started on. All this should be possible without needing to know exactly which thread you started on, as long as you can use the SynchronizationContext, you can get back to it.

The important method of SynchronizationContext is Post, which can make a delegate run in the right context.

Some SynchronizationContexts encapsulate a single thread, like the UI thread. Some encapsulate a particular kind of thread—for example, the thread pool—but can choose any of those threads to post the delegate to. Some don't actually change which thread the code runs on, but are only used for monitoring, like the ASP.NET Synchronization Context.

await and SynchronizationContext

We know that your code before the first await is run by the calling thread, but what about when your method is resumed after the await?

In fact, most of the time, it is also run by the calling thread, despite the fact that the calling thread has probably done other things in between. That makes things very simple for the programmer.

C# uses SynchronizationContext to accomplish this. As we saw previously in "Context" on page 27, when you await a Task, the current SynchronizationContext is stored as part of pausing the method. Then, when it's time for the method to be resumed, the await keyword's infrastructure uses Post to resume the method on the captured SynchronizationContext.

Now, the caveats. The method can resume on a different thread to where it started if:

- The SynchronizationContext was one that has multiple threads, like the thread pool
- The SynchronizationContext was one that doesn't actually switch threads
- There was no current SynchronizationContext when await was reached, for example in a console application
- You configured the Task to not use the SynchronizationContext to resume

Luckily, for UI applications, where being resumed on the same thread is most important, none of these will apply, so you can safely manipulate your UI after an await.

The Lifecycle of an Async Operation

Let's look at a version of the favicon example, working out exactly which thread runs which code. I have written two async methods:

```
async void GetButton_OnClick(...)

async Task<Image> GetFaviconAsync(...)
```

The event handler GetButton_OnClick calls GetFaviconAsync, which in turn calls Web Client.DownloadDataTaskAsync. Here's a diagram of the sequence of events as the methods are executed (Figure 8-1).

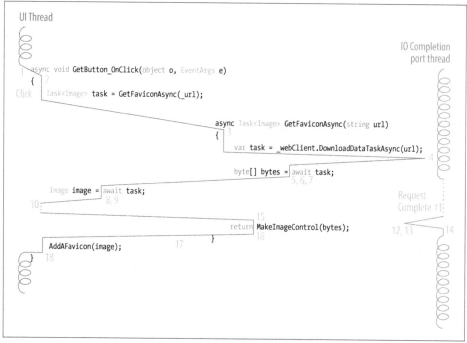

Figure 8-1. lifecycle.png

1. The user clicks the button, so the event handler GetButton_OnClick is queued.

2. The UI thread executes the first half of GetButton_OnClick, including the call to GetFaviconAsync.

3. The UI thread continues into GetFaviconAsync and executes the first half of it, including the call to DownloadDataTaskAsync.

4. The UI thread continues into DownloadDataTaskAsync, which starts the download and returns a Task.

5. The UI thread leaves DownloadDataTaskAsync, and reaches the await in GetFaviconAsyncAsync.

6. The current SynchronizationContext is captured—it's the UI thread.

7. GetFaviconAsync is paused by the await, and the Task from DownloadDataTask Async is told to resume it when done (with the captured SynchronizationContext).

8. The UI thread leaves GetFaviconAsync, which returned a Task, and reaches the await in GetButton_OnClick.

9. Similarly, `GetButton_OnClick` is paused by the `await`.

10. The UI thread leaves `GetButton_OnClick`, and is freed to work on other user actions.

 At this point, we are waiting for the icon to download. This could take a few seconds. Notice the UI thread is free to process other user actions, and the IO completion port thread isn't involved yet. The total number of threads blocked during the operation is zero.

11. The download finishes, so the IO completion port queues the logic in `DownloadDataTaskAsync` to handle that.

12. The IO completion port thread sets the `Task` that was returned from `DownloadData TaskAsync` to complete.

13. The IO completion port thread runs code inside `Task` to handle completion, which calls `Post` on the captured `SynchronizationContext` (the UI thread) to continue.

14. The IO completion port thread is freed to work on other IO.

15. The UI thread finds the `Post`ed instruction and resumes `GetFaviconAsync`, executing the second half of it, to the end.

16. As the UI thread leaves `GetFaviconAsync`, it sets the `Task` that was returned by `GetFaviconAsync` to complete.

17. Because this time, the current `SynchronizationContext` is the same as the captured one, no `Post` is needed, and the UI thread proceeds synchronously.

 This logic is unreliable in WPF, because WPF often creates new `SynchronizationContext` objects. Despite them being equivalent, this makes the TPL think it needs to `Post` again.

18. The UI thread resumes `GetButton_OnClick`, executing the second half of it, to the end.

That was pretty complicated, but I think it's worth seeing each step spelled out. Notice that *every single* line of my code was executed by the UI thread. The IO completion port thread only ran long enough to `Post` an instruction to the UI thread, which ran the second half of both my methods.

Choosing Not to Use SynchronizationContext

Each implementation of `SynchronizationContext` performs `Post` in a different way. Most of them are relatively expensive. To avoid that cost, .NET will not use a `Post` when the captured `SynchronizationContext` is the same as the current at the time of the `Task`'s completion. When this happens, if you look using the debugger, the call stack will be upside-down (ignoring framework code). The deepest method, which from the programmer's point of view is called by other methods, ends up calling the other methods as it completes.

When the `SynchronizationContext` is different, however, an expensive `Post` is needed. In performance-critical code, or in library code where you don't care which thread you use, you might choose not to pay that performance penalty. That's done by calling `ConfigureAwait` on the `Task` before awaiting it. If you do that, it won't `Post` back to the original `SynchronizationContext` when resuming.

```
byte[] bytes = await client.DownloadDataTaskAsync(url).ConfigureAwait(false);
```

`ConfigureAwait` doesn't always do as you might expect, though. It's designed to be a hint to .NET that you don't mind which thread your method resumes on, rather than a strict instruction. What it does depends on is which thread completed the `Task` you're awaiting. If that thread is not important, perhaps from the thread pool, it should continue to execute your code. But if it's an important thread of some kind, .NET will prefer to release it to do other things, and your method will resume on the thread pool instead. .NET uses the current `SynchronizationContext` of the thread to judge whether it's important.

Interacting with Synchronous Code

You are probably already working on an existing application, and while new code you write can be asynchronous using the TAP, you need to communicate with old synchronous code. When you do this, you usually lose the benefits of asynchrony, but it's still worth planning for the future and writing new code in an asynchronous style to be able to make the switch at some point.

Consuming synchronous code from asynchronous code is easy. If given a blocking API, you can just run it on the thread pool and await it, using `Task.Run`. You use a thread, but that's unavoidable.

```
var result = await Task.Run(() => MyOldMethod());
```

Consuming asynchronous code from synchronous code, or implementing a synchronous API, also looks easy, but can have hidden problems. `Task` has a property called `Result`, which blocks waiting for the `Task` to complete. You can use it in similar places to `await`, but without your method needing to be marked `async` or return a `Task`. Again, a thread is wasted. This time the calling thread is used for blocking.

```
var result = AlexsMethodAsync().Result;
```

A word of warning, though: this technique fails whenever it is used from a `SynchronizationContext` with only one thread, like the UI thread. Think about what the UI thread is being asked to do. It is blocked, waiting for the `Task` from `AlexsMethodAsync` to complete. `AlexsMethodAsync` has most likely called another TAP method, and awaited it. When the operation completes, the captured `SynchronizationContext` (the UI thread) is used to `Post` the instruction for `AlexsMethodAsync` to resume. But the UI thread will never pick up that message, because it's still blocking. You've written a deadlock. Luckily, this mistake tends to cause deadlocks that always happen, so aren't too hard to debug.

With care, you can get around the deadlock problem by moving to the thread pool before starting the async code, so that the SynchronizationContext captured is the thread pool rather than the UI thread. This is very ugly, though; it would probably be better to spend the time making the calling code async.

```
var result = Task.Run(() => AlexsMethodAsync()).Result;
```

CHAPTER 9

Exceptions in Async Code

In synchronous code, exceptions work their way up the call stack, back through each method call until they reach either a `try` and `catch` that can catch them, or they leave your code. In async code, particularly after a method has been resumed after an `await`, the current call stack has very little to do with the programmer's intention, and mostly contains framework logic to resume the async method. The exception would be impossible to catch in your calling code, and stack traces wouldn't be very helpful at all, so C# changes the behavior of exceptions to be more useful.

 You can still see the raw call stack in a debugger.

Exceptions in Async Task-Returning Methods

Most async methods you write will return `Task` or `Task<T>`. Chains of these methods, each awaiting the next, are the asynchronous version of the call stack we're familiar with in synchronous code. C# strives to make the behavior of exceptions in these methods feel very similar to working with synchronous methods. In particular, `try..catch` blocks placed around an awaited async method will catch exceptions thrown inside that async method.

```
async Task Catcher()
{
    try
    {
        await Thrower();
    }
    catch (AlexsException)
    {
        // Execution will reach here
    }
}
```

```
async Task Thrower()
{
    await Task.Delay(100);
    throw new AlexsException();
}
```

 Until execution reaches the first await, the synchronous call stack and the chain of async methods are exactly the same. The behavior of exceptions at that point is still changed for consistency, but the change required is much smaller.

To do this, C# catches any exceptions that happen in your async method. When an exception happens, it is placed into the Task that was returned to your caller. The Task becomes *Faulted*. If a method is awaiting the Task when it faults, instead of resuming normally, the method is resumed by an exception thrown from the await.

An exception which has been rethrown by an await is the same object as the original one thrown by the throw statement. It continues to gather a stack trace as it propagates up the call stack, which adds to its existing stack trace. This may surprise you if you've ever tried to rethrow an exception manually, for example in manual asynchronous code, as it represents a new feature in .NET's Exception type.

Here is an example stack trace from a chain of two async methods. My own code is highlighted:

```
System.NullReferenceException: Object reference not set to an instance of an object.
    at FaviconBrowser.MainWindow.<GetFavicon>d__c.MoveNext() in
MainWindow.xaml.cs:line 74
--- End of stack trace from previous location where exception was thrown ---
    at System.Runtime.CompilerServices.TaskAwaiter.ThrowForNonSuccess(Task task)
    at
System.Runtime.CompilerServices.TaskAwaiter.HandleNonSuccessAndDebuggerNotification(T
ask task)
    at System.Runtime.CompilerServices.TaskAwaiter`1.GetResult()
    at FaviconBrowser.MainWindow.<GetButton_OnClick>d__0.MoveNext() in
MainWindow.xaml.cs:line 41
--- End of stack trace from previous location where exception was thrown ---
    at System.Runtime.CompilerServices.AsyncMethodBuilderCore.<ThrowAsync>b__0(Object
state)
    at ... Framework methods
```

The mention of MoveNext has to do with the compiler transformation that we'll look at in Chapter 14. There are a few framework methods between each of mine, but I can still get an impression of the series of my own calls that caused the exception.

Unobserved Exceptions

One important difference between async and synchronous code is where an exception from a called method is thrown. In async methods, it is thrown at the `await`, rather than the actual call to the method. That is apparent if you split up the call and the `await`.

```
// This never throws AlexsException
Task task = Thrower();

try
{
    await task;
}
catch (AlexsException)
{
    // Execution will reach here
}
```

It is now very easy to forget to await an async method, especially one that returned the non-generic `Task` because you don't need any result value from it. Doing this is equivalent to using an empty `catch` block that catches all exceptions and ignores them. This is bad practice, because it tends to result in invalid program state, as well as subtle bugs that happen far away from their cause. Make a point of always awaiting any async method you call to avoid wasting time doing difficult debugging.

 This behavior to ignore exceptions is actually a change from versions of .NET before async was introduced. If you are expecting exceptions from your Task Parallel Library code being rethrown on the finalizer thread, that will no longer happen in .NET 4.5.

Exceptions in Async void Methods

Async methods that return `void` can't be awaited, so their behavior around exceptions must be different. We wouldn't always want their exceptions to be unobserved. Instead, any exceptions that leave an async `void` method are rethrown in the calling thread:

- If there was a `SynchronizationContext` when the async method was called, the exception is `Posted` to it.
- If not, it is thrown on the thread pool.

In most cases, both of these will end the process unless an unhandled exception handler is attached to the appropriate event. That's probably not what you want, which is one reason you should only write an async `void` method for the purpose of being called by external code, or when you can guarantee that it won't throw exceptions.

Fire and Forget

In rare cases, you genuinely don't care whether a method succeeds, and awaiting it would be complex. In that case, my advice is to still return Task, but to pass that Task to a method designed to handle exceptions in it. This extension method works well for me:

```
public static void ForgetSafely(this Task task)
{
    task.ContinueWith(HandleException);
}
```

HandleException is a method that writes any exception to a logging system, like the one in "Creating Your Own Combinators" on page 42.

AggregateException and WhenAll

In the asynchronous world, we have to deal with a situation that just wasn't possible in the synchronous world. A method may throw multiple exceptions at once. This could be, for example, when you use Task.WhenAll to wait for a group of asynchronous operations to complete. Many of them could fail, without any one failure being the first or most important.

WhenAll is just the most common mechanism to produce multiple exceptions; there are plenty of other ways to run multiple operations concurrently using async. So support for multiple exceptions was built directly into Task. Instead of being able to contain an Exception directly, Task contains an AggregateException when it faults. An AggregateException contains a collection of other exceptions.

Because this support is built into Task, when an exception escapes an async method, an AggregateException is created, and the actual exception is added as an inner exception, before being placed in the Task. So mostly, the AggregateException only contains one inner exception, but WhenAll will create an AggregateException with multiple.

 This all happens regardless of whether the exception happens before the first await. Exceptions before the first await could easily have been thrown synchronously, but that would have made them appear in the call to the method rather than the await in the caller, which would have been inconsistent.

At the other end, when the exception is rethrown by an await, we need a compromise. await should throw the same type of exception that was originally thrown in the async method, rather than the AggregateException. So it has no choice but to throw the first inner exception. But after catching it, you can use the Task directly to get the AggregateException, and so the complete list of exceptions.

```
Task<Image[]> allTask = Task.WhenAll(tasks);
try
{
    await allTask;
}
catch
{
    foreach (Exception ex in allTask.Exception.InnerExceptions)
    {
        // Do something with exception
    }
}
```

Throwing Exceptions Synchronously

The TAP recommendation allows methods to throw exceptions synchronously, but only if the exception signifies a mistake in the call to the method, rather than an error encountered while trying to run. We've seen that all async methods catch any exception and place them into the Task, regardless of whether the exception happens before the first await. So if you'd like to throw an exception synchronously, you need to use a trick: using a synchronous method that checks for the mistake before calling the async method.

```
private Task<Image> GetFaviconAsync(string domain)
{
    if (domain == null) throw new ArgumentNullException("domain");

    return GetFaviconAsyncInternal(domain);
}

private async Task<Image> GetFaviconAsyncInternal(string domain)
{
    ...
```

Doing this gives you slightly easier stack traces to interpret. Is it worth the effort? I doubt it. But it was a useful example to help understanding.

finally in Async Methods

Finally, you are allowed to use try..finally in an async method, and it works much like how you'd expect. Before execution leaves the method containing the finally block, the block is guaranteed to run. That's irrespective of whether it leaves by normal execution, which flows through the finally block, or whether an exception happens in the try block.

But that guarantee holds a hidden caveat. With async methods, there's no guarantee that execution will ever leave the method. You can easily write a method that reaches an await, pauses, then is forgotten and garbage collected.

```
async void AlexsMethod()
{
    try
    {
        await DelayForever();
    }
    finally
    {
        // Never happens
    }
}

Task DelayForever()
{
    return new TaskCompletionSource<object>().Task;
}
```

I've used TaskCompletionSource to create a puppet Task, then simply forgotten about it. Because there's no thread in AlexsMethod anymore, there's nothing to mean that it'll ever resume or throw an exception. It will just be garbage collected eventually.

So the guarantee provided by finally is much weaker in async methods.

CHAPTER 10

Parallelism Using Async

Async provides a great opportunity to start making more use of the parallelism of modern machines. The language feature makes previously difficult approaches to structuring programs easier.

For starters, we've already seen we can write simple code that starts multiple long-running operations, for example network requests, which then proceed in parallel. Using tools like WhenAll, async code can be very efficient at this kind of operation—one that doesn't involve local computation. However, when local computation is involved, async on its own doesn't help. Until a source of asynchrony is reached, all the code you write runs synchronously on the calling thread.

await and locks

The simplest way to introduce parallelism is to schedule work in different threads. Task.Run makes this easy, and because it returns a Task, we can treat it like any other long-running operation. But using multiple threads introduces risks of unsafe access to shared objects in memory.

The traditional solution of the lock keyword is more complicated when using async, as we discussed in "lock Blocks" on page 29. The await keyword can't be used in a lock block, so there's no way to prevent execution of conflicting code while you're awaiting something. In fact, it's best to avoid reserving any resources across an await keyword. The whole point of async is that resources are released while awaiting, and as programmers, we need to be aware that anything can happen at that time.

```
lock (sync)
{
    // Prepare for async operation
}

int myNum = await AlexsMethodAsync();
```

```
lock (sync)
{
    // Use result of async operation
}
```

A useful example is the UI thread. There is only one UI thread, so in a way it acts as a lock. As long as you know that your code runs on the UI thread, only one line of your code is ever executing at once. But even then, anything can happen while awaiting. If you started a network operation because the user pressed a button, they are at liberty to press another button while your code is awaiting. That's exactly the point of async in UI applications: the UI is responsive, and will do whatever the user asks, even if it's dangerous.

But at least with async, we can choose the points in the program where other things can take place. We have to learn to put `awaits` at safe places, and expect the state of the world to have changed after resuming. Sometimes that means making a second, seemingly pointless, check about whether to proceed.

```
if (DataInvalid())
{
    Data d = await GetNewData();

    // Anything could have happened in the await
    if (DataInvalid())
    {
        SetNewData(d);
    }
}
```

Actors

I said the UI thread is like a lock, simply because there's only one of it. In fact, a better way of putting it is to say it's an actor. An actor is a thread which has responsibility for a particular set of data, and no other thread may access the data. In this case, only the UI thread may access the data that makes up the UI. That means it's much easier to maintain safety in UI code, the only place where anything could happen is an `await`.

More generally, you can build programs from components which operate in one thread and look after some data. This is actors programming. It enables you to make use of parallel computers, as each actor can use a different core. It's effective for general programming, where the different components have state that needs to be maintained safely.

 Other techniques, for example dataflow programming, are very effective for *embarrassingly parallel* problems, where there are many computations that don't depend on each other and can be parallelized in an obvious way. Actors are the right choice when this isn't obvious.

At first, programming using actors may sound a lot like programming using locks. They share the concept of only one thread being allowed access to one piece of data. But the difference is that one thread may never be in multiple actors at once. Instead of a thread holding the resources of one actor while it executes code in another actor, it must make an asynchronous call. The calling actor is then free to do other things while waiting.

Actors are an inherently more scalable way of programming than using locks with shared memory. Multiple cores accessing a single memory address space is a model that is becoming increasingly detached from reality. If you've ever programmed with locks, you'll know the pain of deadlocks and race conditions that are so easy to introduce in locking code.

Using Actors in C#

Of course, you can use an actors style of programming manually, but there are libraries that make it simpler. NAct (*http://code.google.com/p/n-act/*) is one that makes full use of async in C# to allow ordinary objects to become actors, so that calls to them are moved onto their own thread. It does this with a proxy that wraps the object, turning it into an actor.

Let's look at an example. Perhaps I am implementing a cryptography service that needs a series of pseudo-random numbers to use while encrypting a stream of data. There are two kinds of compute-intensive work here, so I'd like to be able to do them in parallel:

- Generating the random numbers
- Using them to encrypt the stream

We'll just look at implementing the random number generator actor. NAct needs an interface which we'll implement, and then NAct will create a proxy for.

```
public interface IRndGenerator : IActor
{
    Task<int> GetNextNumber();
}
```

The interface must implement `IActor`, which is just an empty marker interface. All the methods of the interface must return one of the asynchronous compatible return types:

- void
- Task
- Task<*T*>

Then, we can implement the generator class itself.

```
class RndGenerator : IRndGenerator
{
    public async Task<int> GetNextNumber()
    {
        // Generate a secure random number - slow
        ...
        return num;
    }
}
```

The only surprise here is that there's nothing surprising. It's just a normal class. To use it, we must construct one, and give it to NAct to wrap up, creating an actor.

```
IRndGenerator rndActor = ActorWrapper.WrapActor(new RndGenerator());

Task<int> nextTask = rndActor.GetNextNumber();
foreach (var chunk in stream)
{
    int rndNum = await nextTask;

    // Get started on the next number
    nextTask = rndActor.GetNextNumber();

    // Use rndNum to encode chunk - slow
    ...
}
```

Each iteration through the encoding I await a random number, then begin the process of generating the next before doing the slow work myself. Because rndActor is an actor, NAct will return the Task immediately, and run the generation in the RndGenerator's thread. Now, the two kinds of computation will proceed in parallel, making better use of the CPU. The async language features have made this previously difficult programming style very natural.

This isn't the place for more details about how to use NAct, but I hope I've given you enough to see how simple the actors model is to use. Other features like firing events on the correct thread, and intelligently sharing threads between idle actors mean that it scales to real-world systems.

Task Parallel Library Dataflow

Another useful tool for parallel programming that is easier to use with C# async is dataflow programming. In this model, you specify a series of operations that need to happen to input data, and the system will parallelize them automatically. Microsoft provides a library for this called TPL Dataflow, which is available on NuGet (*https://nuget.org/packages/Microsoft.Tpl.Dataflow*).

Dataflow programming is a particularly useful technique when the most performance critical part of your program is a data transformation. There's nothing stopping you using both actors and dataflow programming, where one actor which has a heavy computational load uses dataflow to parallelize it.

TPL Dataflow is concerned with pushing messages between *blocks*. To create a dataflow network, you string together blocks which implement two interfaces:

ISourceBlock<*T*>
Something which you can ask for messages of type *T*

ITargetBlock<*T*>
Something which you can give messages

The ISourceBlock<*T*> interface has a method LinkTo, which takes an ITargetBlock<*T*> and ties them together, so every message produced by the ISourceBlock<*T*> is given to the ITargetBlock<*T*>. Most blocks implement both interfaces, perhaps with different type parameters, so that they consume one kind of message and produce another.

While you can implement these interfaces yourself, it's much more normal to use the built-in blocks, for example:

ActionBlock<*T*>
When you construct an ActionBlock<*T*>, you pass it a delegate, and it performs that delegate for every message. ActionBlock<*T*> only implements ITargetBlock<*T*>.

TransformBlock<*TIn, TOut*>
Similarly, you pass a delegate to the constructor, but this time the delegate is a function that returns a value. That value becomes a message passed to the next block. TransformBlock<*TIn, TOut*> implements both ITargetBlock<*TIn*> and ISourceBlock<*TOut*>. It is the parallel version of a LINQ Select.

JoinBlock<*T1, T2,...*>
This joins multiple input streams into a single output stream of tuples.

There are many other built-in blocks, and with them you can implement any conveyor-belt style computation. Out of the box, the blocks act as a pipeline in parallel, but each block will only process one message at a time. That's fine if most of your blocks take a similar length of time, but if an individual stage is slower than the rest, you can configure ActionBlock<*T*>s and TransformBlock<*TIn, TOut*> to work in parallel within the individual block, effectively splitting itself into many identical blocks and sharing the work.

TPL dataflow is improved by async because the delegates passed to `ActionBlock<T>`s and `TransformBlock<TIn, TOut>`s can be async, and can return `Task` or `Task<T>` respectively. When those delegates involve long-running remote operations, this is very important, as those long running operations can be run in parallel without wasting threads. Also, when interacting with dataflow blocks from the outside, it's useful to do so in an asynchronous way, so there are TAP methods like the `SendAsync` extension method on `ITargetBlock<T>` to make that easy.

CHAPTER 11

Unit Testing Async Code

I'd like to look briefly at how to unit test async code. The simplest approach doesn't work well, but it can be easy to write good tests that call async methods, depending on support from your unit test framework.

The Problem with Unit Testing in Async

Async methods return quickly, usually returning a Task that completes at some point in the future. To consume them, we'd normally use await, so let's experiment with that approach in a unit test.

```
[TestMethod]
public async void AlexsTest()
{
    int x = await AlexsMethod();
    Assert.AreEqual(3, x);
}
```

To allow us to use await, I've also marked my test method async. But that has a very important side effect. Now, the test method also returns quickly and completes at some point in the future. In fact, the test method returned without throwing any exceptions as soon as it reaches the await, so the test framework, in this case MSTest, marks it as a pass.

Because the test method is async void, any exceptions that happen in it are rethrown on the calling SynchronizationContext, where they are either ignored, or cause an unrelated future test to fail.

The real danger here is that all your tests will appear to pass, irrespective of the actual result.

Writing Working Async Tests Manually

One way to avoid this problem is to avoid making your test methods async. Instead, we have to wait synchronously for the result of any async calls they make.

```
[TestMethod]
public void AlexsTest()
{
    int x = AlexsMethod().Result;
    Assert.AreEqual(3, x);
}
```

The `Result` property waits for the `Task` to complete before proceeding, blocking the thread. This works fine, and the test can now fail if it needs to. If an exception is thrown during `AlexsMethod`, it will be rethrown by `Result`, although unlike when rethrown by an `await`, it will still be wrapped by an `AggregateException`.

By now, it should feel ugly to use the blocking `Result` of a `Task`. It is a dangerous thing to do, as we saw in "Interacting with Synchronous Code" on page 52 when in a single-threaded `SynchronizationContext`. Luckily, no popular desktop test frameworks use a single-threaded `SynchronizationContext` by default. Still, this solution wastes a thread and doesn't perform optimally because of it.

Using Unit Test Framework Support

Some unit test frameworks support async explicitly. They allow you to create test methods which return `Task`, so you can write async test methods. The framework will wait for the `Task` to complete before marking it as a pass and moving onto the next test.

 At the time of writing, xUnit.net and MSTest support this style. I expect the other popular frameworks will add it in time, or make it possible with a small extension.

```
[TestMethod]
public async Task AlexsTest()
{
    int x = await AlexsMethod();
    Assert.AreEqual(3, x);
}
```

This is arguably the neatest way to write unit tests for async code, pushing the responsibility for threads into the testing framework.

CHAPTER 12

Async in ASP.NET Applications

The majority of .NET developers write web applications. Async brings some new performance possibilities to web server code, so we'll look at how to use async within web applications.

Advantages of Asynchronous Web Server Code

On a web server, responsiveness during a request isn't an issue in the same way that it is in UI code. Instead, the performance of a web server is measured by its throughput and latency, and how consistent those are.

Asynchronous code, on a heavily loaded web server, requires fewer threads than synchronous code to do the same amount of work. Each thread has a large memory overhead, and the bottleneck for web servers is often memory capacity. When memory is scarce, the garbage collector has to run more often, and usually does more work in total. If the memory used doesn't fit into the physical memory of the server, it has to be paged to a disk, which can be very slow if the memory is used again soon.

It's been possible to write asynchronous web server code in ASP.NET since version 2.0, but doing so was difficult without language support. For most people, the option to add more servers and load balance between them was more cost effective. With C# 5 and .NET 4.5, it becomes easy enough that it's worth everyone taking advantage of the efficiency.

Using Async in ASP.NET MVC 4

ASP.NET MVC 4 and later, when run on .NET 4.5 or later, has full support for the Task-based Asynchronous Pattern, so we can use async methods. The important place for asynchrony in an MVC application is the controller. You can simply use an async method to return a `Task<ActionResult>` from your controller methods:

```
public class HomeController : Controller
{
    public async Task<ActionResult> Index()
    {
        ViewBag.Message = await GetMessageAsync();

        return View();
    }
    ...
```

This relies on the fact that the long-running requests you want to make provide an asynchronous API for you to call. Many object relational mappers (ORMs) don't support asynchronous calls yet, but the .NET framework's `SqlConnection` API does.

Using Async in Older Versions of ASP.NET MVC

Before MVC 4, the support for asynchronous controllers isn't based on the TAP, and is more involved. Here is a way to adapt an MVC 4 style TAP controller method to the pattern used in older versions of MVC.

```
public class HomeController : AsyncController
{
    public void IndexAsync()
    {
        AsyncManager.OutstandingOperations.Increment();
        Task<ActionResult> task = IndexTaskAsync();
        task.ContinueWith(_ =>
            {
                AsyncManager.Parameters["result"] = task.Result;
                AsyncManager.OutstandingOperations.Decrement();
            });
    }

    public ActionResult IndexCompleted(ActionResult result)
    {
        return result;
    }

    private async Task<ActionResult> IndexTaskAsync()
    {
    ...
```

First, the controller must derive from `AsyncController` rather than `Controller`, which enables it to use an asynchronous pattern. That pattern means that for every action, there are two methods, one named *Action*Async and one named *Action*Completed. `AsyncManager` controls the lifetime of an asynchronous request. When `Outstanding Operations` is decremented to zero, *Action*Completed is called. We consume the `Task` manually using `ContinueWith`, and pass the result to the *Action*Completed method with a dictionary called `Parameters`.

I've neglected exceptions in this example to keep it simpler. All in all, very ugly, but once this is done, you can use async as you would normally.

Using Async in ASP.NET Web Forms

Standard ASP.NET and Web Forms don't have a version separate to the .NET framework version on which they run. In .NET 4.5, ASP.NET supports async void methods on your Page, for example Page_Load.

```
protected async void Page_Load(object sender, EventArgs e)
{
    Title = await GetTitleAsync();
}
```

You may find this an odd implementation. How does ASP.NET know when the async void method completes? It would have made more sense to return a Task, which ASP.NET could then wait for before rendering the page, much like in MVC 4. However, presumably for backward compatibility reasons, it requires that methods return void. Instead, ASP.NET uses a special SynchronizationContext that keeps track of asynchronous operations and only moves on when they are all completed.

Take care when running asynchronous code in the ASP.NET Synchronization Context, because it is single-threaded. If you use a blocking wait on a Task, for example the Result property, the chances are that you will cause a deadlock, as deeper awaits won't be able to use the SynchronizationContext to resume.

Async in WinRT Applications

For those who aren't already familiar with WinRT, I'll give a brief overview of the technology before moving on to explore how async and WinRT work together.

What Is WinRT?

WinRT (or Windows Runtime) is a group of APIs that are used in Windows 8 applications that run on Windows 8 and Windows RT for ARM processors. One of the design goals of the WinRT APIs is responsiveness, achieved by asynchronous programming. All methods that could take longer than 50ms are asynchronous.

It is designed to be used uniformly from three completely different technology stacks: .NET, JavaScript, and native code (usually C++). To achieve this, the APIs are all defined in a common metadata format called WinMD. Each of the languages can then compile against the WinMD definition of the API, without any need for a language-specific wrapper. This system is called projection, where each compiler or interpreter projects the WinRT type to be used as a normal type in the language.

 WinMD is based on the .NET assembly metadata format, so the constructs that are available are very similar to .NET: classes interfaces, methods, properties, attributes, etc. There are differences, though; for example, generic types are legal, but generic methods aren't.

The majority of WinRT is implemented in native code, but you can also write WinRT components in C#, which you or others can then consume from any of the supported languages.

Because the WinRT interfaces are not .NET, the API provided by your WinRT component can't use a lot of .NET types. Many collection interfaces are projected automatically; for example, `IList<T>`. However, `Task` is not, because it has too much .NET-specific behavior.

IAsyncAction and IAsyncOperation<T>

These two interfaces are the WinRT equivalents of Task and Task<T> respectively. WinRT asynchronous methods use a pattern similar to the Task-based Asynchronous Pattern, but return IAsyncAction or IAsyncOperation<T>. The two interfaces work very similarly to each other, so for the rest of this chapter, I mean both when I refer to either one.

Here is an example method in the WinRT type SyndicationClient which gets an RSS feed.

```
IAsyncOperation<SyndicationFeed> RetrieveFeedAsync(Uri uri)
```

 Remember that IAsyncAction and IAsyncOperation<T> are not .NET interfaces, they are WinMD interfaces. The distinction is a little confusing, because they can be used from C# as if they were normal .NET interfaces.

Just like TAP methods, this kind of WinRT method begins immediately and returns the IAsyncOperation<T>, which acts as a promise of a future SyndicationFeed. The await keyword can be used on IAsyncOperation<T> in exactly the same way as Task, so you can use RetrieveFeedAsync like this:

```
SyndicationFeed feed = await rssClient.RetrieveFeedAsync(url);
```

await can be used on any type which contains a specific pattern of methods that provide the behavior needed. Task has those methods, but IAsyncOperation<T> doesn't. However, the pattern can be fulfilled using extension methods, so .NET provides those extension methods on IAsyncOperation<T> to make await work.

You may need access to a Task representing the asynchronous WinRT call; for example, to pass to a combinator like Task.WhenAll or to use ConfigureAwait. To create one, there is another extension method on IAsyncOperation<T> called AsTask:

```
Task<SyndicationFeed> task = rssClient.RetrieveFeedAsync(url).AsTask();
```

Using AsTask, you get a normal Task, which you can use in any way you like.

Cancellation

The WinRT version of the TAP chose a different design for cancellation. Whereas in .NET TAP, we pass a CancellationToken as an extra parameter, in WinRT cancellation is built into the returned IAsyncOperation<T>.

```
IAsyncOperation<SyndicationFeed> op = rssClient.RetrieveFeedAsync(url);
op.Cancel();
```

Because it's built in, all asynchronous WinRT methods expose the ability to cancel. Whether they all actually stop when Cancel is called is a different question, and I imagine some don't.

 This design has benefits and disadvantages when compared to the CancellationToken approach, so it's not surprising that one was chosen for TAP while the other was chosen for WinRT. CancellationToken makes it easier to propagate a single CancellationToken to many methods, while putting cancellation into the returned promise type makes the API cleaner.

You shouldn't normally use this Cancel method directly, though, because the AsTask extension method has an overload that takes a standard .NET CancellationToken and hooks everything up for you.

```
... = await rssClient.RetrieveFeedAsync(url).AsTask(cancellationToken);
```

Now you can use CancellationTokenSource as normal.

Progress

Again, progress in asynchronous WinRT methods uses a different design to the TAP. In WinRT, the ability to return progress is built into the returned promise type. Progress, however, is optional, so methods that can give progress updates return specialized interfaces:

- IAsyncActionWithProgress<*TProgress*>
- IAsyncOperationWithProgress<*T, TProgress*>

These correspond in the obvious way to IAsyncAction and IAsyncOperation<*T*>, and are similar to those interfaces, but add an event that fires when progress changes.

The best way to subscribe to that progress is, again, to use an overload of AsTask, which takes a standard .NET IProgress<*T*> and hooks it up for you.

```
... = await rssClient.RetrieveFeedAsync(url).AsTask(progress);
```

Of course, there's also an overload that takes both a CancellationToken and an IProgress<*T*>, in case you need both.

Providing Asynchronous Methods in a WinRT Component

The power of WinRT comes from the way that the libraries provided can be used equally easily from any of the supported languages. If you write your own libraries to run under WinRT, you might want to take advantage of that same power by compiling your library as a WinRT component rather than a .NET assembly.

That's very easy to do in C#, but the public interface of your component must only use types that are either WinMD types or automatically projected by the compiler to WinMD types. Again, Task is neither of these, so we need to return an IAsyncOperation<T> instead.

```
public IAsyncOperation<int> GetTheIntAsync()
{
    return GetTheIntTaskAsync().AsAsyncOperation();
}

private async Task<int> GetTheIntTaskAsync()
{
    ...
```

Extension methods provided by .NET make life easy once again. AsAsyncOperation does exactly what we need in the simple case, turning a Task<T> into an IAsync Operation<T>. Correspondingly, AsAsyncAction will turn a Task into an IAsyncAction.

 As a bonus, AsTask and AsAsyncOperation are aware of each other, and can detect whether both the implementer and consumer of the WinMD method are .NET code. If they are, the original Task is returned directly, improving performance.

When cancellation or progress are needed, AsAsyncOperation isn't powerful enough. TAP methods need a CancellationToken or IProgress<T> as they are called, so an extension method on Task can't possibly handle them. To convert between the different models, we need a more complex tool called AsyncInfo.Run.

```
public IAsyncOperation<int> GetTheIntAsync()
{
    return AsyncInfo.Run(cancellationToken =>
        GetTheIntTaskAsync(cancellationToken));
}

private async Task<int> GetTheIntTaskAsync(CancellationToken ct)
{
    ...
```

AsyncInfo.Run takes a delegate, which allows it to pass a CancellationToken, an IPro gress<T>, or both, to your lambda. You can then pass those into your TAP method. You can think of AsAsyncOperation as a shortcut to the simplest overload of AsyncInfo.Run, whose delegate takes no parameters.

CHAPTER 14

The Async Compiler Transform—
in Depth

Async is implemented in the C# compiler with some help from the .NET framework base class libraries. The runtime itself didn't need any changes to support async. That means `await` is implemented by a transformation to something that we could have written ourselves in earlier versions of C#. We can use a decompiler like .NET Reflector to take a look at the generated code.

As well as being interesting, understanding the generated code is helpful for debugging, performance analysis, and other diagnostics on async code.

The stub Method

The async method is replaced by a stub method. The first thing that happens when you call an async method is that the stub method runs. Let's look at this simple async method as an example:

```
public async Task<int> AlexsMethod()
{
    int foo = 3;
    await Task.Delay(500);
    return foo;
}
```

The stub method generated by the compiler looks like this:

```
public Task<int> AlexsMethod()
{
    <AlexsMethod>d__0 stateMachine = new <AlexsMethod>d__0();
    stateMachine.<>4__this = this;
    stateMachine.<>t__builder = AsyncTaskMethodBuilder<int>.Create();
    stateMachine.<>1__state = -1;
    stateMachine.<>t__builder.Start<<AlexsMethod>d__0>(ref stateMachine);
    return stateMachine.<>t__builder.Task;
}
```

I've manually improved the names of the variables to make it easier to understand.

As we saw in "Async, Method Signatures, and Interfaces" on page 22, the `async` keyword has no effect on how the method is used from the outside. That becomes obvious when you see that the signature of the stub method is always just the same as the original async method, but without the `async` keyword.

You'll notice that none of my original code is in the stub method. Most of the stub method consists of initializing the variables of a struct, called `<AlexsMethod>d__0`. That struct is a state machine and is where all the hard work is done. The stub method calls a method `Start`, then it returns a `Task`. To understand what is happening, we need to look inside the state machine struct itself.

The State Machine Struct

The compiler generates a struct that acts as a state machine and contains all the code of my original method. It does this so that there is an object capable of representing the state of the method, which can be stored when execution reaches an `await`. Remember that when we reach an `await`, everything about where we are in the method is remembered, so it can be restored when the method is resumed.

Although it would be feasible for the compiler to go through and store each local variable of your method when it pauses, it would be a lot of generated code. A better way is to change all the local variables of your method into member variables of a type, so we can just store the instance of the type and all the local variables will automatically be kept as well. That's exactly what this struct is for.

> The state machine is a struct rather than a class for performance reasons. It means that when an async method completes synchronously, it doesn't need to be allocated to the heap. Unfortunately, being a struct makes it harder for us to reason about.

The state machine is generated as an inner struct of the type containing the async method. That makes it easy to work out which method it was generated from, but is primarily so it can access the private members of your type.

Let's look at the state machine struct `<AlexsMethod>d__0` generated for our example. For now, we'll concentrate on the member variables:

```
public int <>1__state;
public int <foo>5__1;
public AlexsClass <>4__this;
public AsyncTaskMethodBuilder<int> <>t__builder;
private object <>t__stack;
private TaskAwaiter <>u__$awaiter2;
```

All the variables have angle brackets in their names. That's just to mark them as compiler generated. It is important in other compiler generated code, which has to coexist with user code because angle brackets can't be used in variables in valid C#. Here, it's not really necessary.

First, the state variable, `<>1__state`, is a place to store the `await` we have reached. Before we reach any `await`, its value is `-1`. Each `await` in the original method is numbered, and when the method is paused, the number of the `await` to resume from is written to the state variable.

Next is `<foo>5__1`, which stores the value of my original variable `foo`. We'll see soon that all accesses to my `foo` have been replaced by accesses to this member variable instead.

Then, we have `<>4__this`. This only appears in the state machine for non-static async methods and contains the object that the async method was part of. In a way, you can think of `this` as just another local variable in a method, which happens to be used implicitly when you access other members of the same object. After the async transformation, it needs to be stored and used explicitly, because my code has been moved from its original object to the state machine struct.

The `AsyncTaskMethodBuilder` is a helper type that contains the logic that all of these state machines share. This is what creates the `Task` that is returned by the stub method. In fact, its job is very similar to `TaskCompletionSource`, in that it creates a puppet `Task` to return, which it can complete later. The difference from `TaskCompletionSource` is that it is optimized for async methods, and uses tricks like being a struct rather than a class for performance.

Async methods that return `void` use `AsyncVoidMethodBuilder` as their helper, while async methods that return `Task<T>` use a generic version, `AsyncTaskMethodBuilder<T>`.

The stack variable, `<>t__stack`, is used for `await`s which are part of a larger expression. .NET intermediate language (IL) is a stack-based language, so complex expressions are built of small instructions which manipulate a stack of values. When the `await` is in the middle of that kind of complex expression, the current values in the stack are placed in this stack variable, inside a `Tuple` if there is more than one.

Finally, the `TaskAwaiter` variable is temporary storage for the object that helps the `await` keyword to sign up for notification when the `Task` completes.

The MoveNext Method

The state machine always has a method called MoveNext, where all your original code ends up. This method is called both when the method is first run and when we resume from an await. Even for the simplest async method, it is overwhelmingly complex to look at, so I'll try to explain the transformation as a series of steps. I'll also skip over some less relevant details, so this description is not completely accurate in a lot of places.

 The method was called MoveNext originally because of its similarity to the MoveNext methods generated by iterator blocks in earlier versions of C#. Those implement IEnumerable in a single method using the yield return keyword. The state machine system used there is similar to the async state machine, although simpler.

Your Code

The first step is to copy your code into the MoveNext method. Remember that any accesses to variables need to change to point at the new member variable of the state machine instead. Where the await was, I'll leave a gap which we'll need to fill later.

```
<foo>5__1 = 3;
Task t = Task.Delay(500);
Logic to await t goes here
return <foo>5__1;
```

Transforming Returns to Completions

Every return statement in the original code needs to be converted to code that will complete the Task that was returned by the stub method. In fact, MoveNext returns void, so our return foo; isn't even valid.

```
<>t__builder.SetResult(<foo>5__1);
return;
```

Of course, after completing the Task, we use return; to exit from MoveNext.

Get to the Right Place in the Method

Because MoveNext is called to resume from each await, as well as when the method is first started, we need to start by jumping to the right place in the method. This is done using IL similar to that generated by a switch statement, as if we are switching on the state.

```
    switch (<>1__state)
    {
        case -1: // Right at the start of the method
            <foo>5__1 = 3;
            Task t = Task.Delay(500);
            Logic to await t goes here
        case 0: // There's only one await, so it is number 0
            <>t__builder.SetResult(<foo>5__1);
            return;
    }
```

Pausing the Method for the await

This is where we use the TaskAwaiter to sign up for notification of when the Task we're awaiting completes. We need to update the state to make sure we resume at the right point. Once everything is signed up and ready, we return, releasing the thread to do other things as a good asynchronous method must.

```
    ...
        <foo>5__1 = 3;
        <>u__$awaiter2 = Task.Delay(500).GetAwaiter();
        <>1__state = 0;
        <>t__builder.AwaitUnsafeOnCompleted(<>u__$awaiter2, this);
        return;
    case 0:
    ...
```

The AsyncTaskMethodBuilder is also involved in signing up for notification, and the process is complicated. This is where advanced features of await are organized, like capturing a SynchronizationContext to use to resume. But the end result is easy to understand. When the Task completes, our MoveNext method will be called again.

Resuming after the Await

Once the Task we were awaiting completes, and we're back at the right point of the MoveNext method, we still need to get the result of the Task before proceeding with my code. In this example, we are using a non-generic Task, so there's no value to read into a variable. But there's still the chance that the Task is faulted, and an exception needs to be thrown. Calling GetResult on the TaskAwaiter does all this.

```
    ...
    case 0:
        <>u__$awaiter2.GetResult();
        <>t__builder.SetResult(<foo>5__1);
    ...
```

Completing Synchronously

Remember that when await is used on a Task that already completed synchronously, execution should proceed without having to pause and resume the method. To achieve that, we need to check whether the Task is completed before returning. If it is, we just use `goto case` to jump to the right place to continue.

```
...
<>u__$awaiter2 = Task.Delay(500).GetAwaiter();
if (<>u__$awaiter2.IsCompleted)
{
    goto case 0;
}
<>1__state = 0;
...
```

 The great thing about compiler-generated code is that no one has to maintain it, so you can use `goto` as much as you like. I had previously never heard of `goto case` statements, and that's probably a good thing.

Catching Exceptions

If an exception is thrown during the execution of your async method, and there's no `try..catch` block to handle it, the compiler-generated code will catch it instead. It does this so it can set the returned Task to faulted, rather than letting the exception escape. Remember that the MoveNext method can be called from either the original caller of the async method, or by an awaited Task that has completed, possibly via a Synchroniza tionContext. None of these are expecting an exception to escape.

```
try
{
    ... Whole method
}
catch (Exception e)
{
    <>t__builder.SetException(<>t__ex);
    return;
}
```

More Complicated Code

My example was very simple. The MoveNext method becomes much more complicated if you introduce features like:

- `try..catch..finally` blocks
- Branches (`if` and `switch`)
- Loops
- Using `await` in the middle of an expression

The compiler transform does handle all of these constructs correctly, so as the programmer, you don't need to worry about how complex they would be.

I would encourage you to use a decompiler to look at a MoveNext method for one of your own async methods. Try to spot the simplifications I've made in this description, and work out how more complex code is transformed.

Writing Custom Awaitable Types

Task is an awaitable type, in that you can apply await to it. As we saw in "IAsyncAction and IAsyncOperation<T>" on page 74, other types can also be awaitable, for example the WinRT type IAsyncAction. In fact, although you should never need to, it's possible to write your own awaitable types.

To be awaitable, the type needs to provide the abilities used by the MoveNext method that we just saw. First, it needs to have a method called GetAwaiter:

```
class MyAwaitableClass
{
    public AlexsAwaiter GetAwaiter()
    {
        ...
```

That GetAwaiter method can be an extension method, which is a really important flexibility. For example, IAsyncAction doesn't have a GetAwaiter method, because it is from WinRT, and WinRT has no concept of awaitable types. IAsyncAction becomes awaitable because an extension method GetAwaiter is provided by .NET.

Then, the type returned by GetAwaiter has to follow a specific pattern in order that MyAwaitableClass is considered awaitable. The minimum required is:

- It implements INotifyCompletion, so it contains a method void OnCompleted(Action handler), which signs up for notification of completion
- It contains a property bool IsCompleted { get; }, which is used to check for synchronous completion
- It contains a method T GetResult(), which returns the result of the operation, and throws any exceptions

The return type T of GetResult can be void, like it is for Task. Alternatively, it can be a real type, like it is for Task<T>. Only in the second case will the compiler let you use the await as an expression—for example, by assigning the result to a variable.

Here's what AlexsAwaiter might look like:

```
class AlexsAwaiter : INotifyCompletion
{
    public bool IsCompleted
    {
        get
        {
            ...
        }
    }

    public void OnCompleted(Action continuation)
    {
        ...
    }

    public void GetResult()
    {
        ...
    }
}
```

It's important to remember that TaskCompletionSource exists, and that it's usually a much better option when you need to turn something asynchronous into something awaitable. Task has a lot of useful features and you don't want to miss out on them.

Interacting with the Debugger

You might think that after the compiler has moved your code around so much, the Visual Studio debugger would have trouble making sense of it to show you what's happening. In fact, the debugging experience is very good. This is primarily achieved by the compiler linking the lines in your source code with the parts of the MoveNext method that were converted from your code. This mapping, stored in the .pdb file, means that these features of the debugger work normally:

- Setting breakpoints
- Stepping between lines that don't include an await
- Viewing the correct line where an exception was thrown

However, if you look closely while stopped at a breakpoint after an await in an async method, you can see that the compiler transform has taken place. The clues are:

- The name of the current method will appear to be MoveNext in some places. The Call Stack window translates it back to the original method name successfully, but Intellitrace doesn't.
- The Call Stack window shows that the call stack contains frames from the TPL infrastructure, followed by *[Resuming Async Method]*, followed by your method.

The real magic is stepping through the code. In a heroic effort, the Visual Studio debugger can correctly *Step Over (F10)* an `await`, despite the method continuing an indeterminate time in the future on an indeterminate thread. You can see the infrastructure that went into this ability in `AsyncTaskMethodBuilder`, which has a property called `ObjectIdForDebugger`. The debugger can also *Step Out (Shift+F11)* from an async method, which will take you to just after the `await`, which is currently waiting for it to complete.

CHAPTER 15

The Performance of Async Code

When you choose to use async code, you're probably thinking about performance. Whether that's the responsiveness of a UI application, the throughput of a server, or enabling parallelism using actors, you need to know that the change is actually going to be worthwhile.

To think about the performance of async code, you have to look at it in comparison to the alternatives that are relevant in each situation. In this chapter, we will consider:

- Situations with a long-running operation that has the potential to be executed asynchronously
- Situations with no long-running operation, where there's no opportunity to execute asynchronously
- Comparisons of async code against standard code, which blocks during long-running operations
- Comparisons of async code against manual asynchronous code

We'll also discuss a few optimizations that can be useful if you find that the extra overhead of the async machinery is causing a performance problem in your application.

Measuring Async Overhead

The machinery of async methods inevitably uses more processor cycles than the equivalent synchronous code, and the switches between threads add extra latency. It's impossible to measure the performance overhead of an async method exactly. The performance in your application depends on what other threads are doing, cache behavior, and other unpredictable factors. There's also a distinction between processor usage and added latency, since an asynchronous system can easily add time to an operation without using the CPU, while a request is waiting in a queue to be executed.

So I'll just give you an order of magnitude analysis to the nearest factor of 10. I'll use the cost of a normal method call as a baseline for comparisons. My laptop can call a method roughly 100 million times per second.

Async Versus Blocking for a Long-Running Operation

The usual reason to use async code is a long-running operation that you can execute asynchronously, freeing up resources. In UI code, unless that operation is sure to be quick, it's usually worth using async to keep the UI responsive. In server-side code, the trade-off is much more subtle, as you are trading the extra memory footprint of blocked threads for the extra processor overhead of the async methods.

The overhead of an async method which actually executes asynchronously depends entirely on whether it needs to switch threads using SynchronizationContext.Post. If it does, the overhead is dominated by the thread switch it performs as it resumes. That means that the current SynchronizationContext makes a big difference. I've measured this overhead by running this method, which does nothing but await Task.Yield, which always completes asynchronously:

```
async Task AlexsMethod()
{
    await Task.Yield();
}
```

Table 15-1. Overhead to execute and resume an async method

SynchronizationContext	Cost (compared to an empty method)
No Post needed	100
Thread pool	100
Windows forms	1,000
WPF	1,000
ASP.NET	1,000

Whether we need to pay to switch threads depends on the SynchronizationContext of the original caller, as well as the SynchronizationContext of the thread which completed our Task.

- If they are the same, there's no need to Post to the original Synchronization Context, and the method can be resumed by the thread that completed the Task, synchronously, as part of completing the Task.

- If the original caller had a SynchronizationContext, but not the same one as the completion thread, we need to do the Post, incurring the high cost shown in the table. This also happens if the completion thread has no SynchronizationContext.

- If the original caller had no SynchronizationContext—for example, in a console application, then what happens depends on the SynchronizationContext of the completion thread. If there is a `SynchronizationContext`, .NET assumes that the thread is important and schedules our method to resume on the thread pool. If the completion thread has no `SynchronizationContext`, or just the default thread pool one, it resumes our method on the same thread, synchronously.

In reality, the .NET thread pool is so fast that the overhead of switching to it doesn't even show up in my order of magnitude numbers, when compared to resuming the method in the same thread. Given that, you don't really need to worry about the `SynchronizationContext` of the completion thread.

These rules mean that a chain of async methods will tend to incur one expensive thread switch, as the deepest method resumes. After that, the `SynchronizationContext`s will be the same, and the rest of the methods can resume cheaply. The thread switch in a UI context is one of the most expensive. However, in a UI application, the user's experience is so bad if you don't use async code that you don't have a real choice. If you are doing a network request that takes 500ms, it's worth paying another millisecond for a responsive UI.

Unfortunately, WPF recreates `SynchronizationContext` objects often, so in a WPF context, a deep stack of async methods incurs the large cost of a WPF `Post` for every method resumed. Windows forms and Windows 8 applications don't suffer from the same problem.

The trade-off requires more thought in server-side code—for example, ASP.NET applications. Whether async code is worthwhile depends largely on whether your server has a bottleneck in memory usage, because the biggest cost of using many threads is memory. Many factors can cause your synchronous application to consume memory faster than it consumes processor time, including:

- You call long-running operations that take a relatively long time
- You parallelize long-running operations by using extra threads
- Many requests call through to the long-running operations, rather than being served by in-memory caches
- Generating the response doesn't require very much processor time

The only way to really know is to measure the memory usage of your server. If the memory usage is a problem, and the memory is being used by too many threads, async is a good solution. It uses a little more CPU, but when the server is running out of memory and has plenty of CPU, that's no problem.

Remember that while async methods will always use more processor time than synchronous methods, the difference is really quite small, and can easily be dominated by anything else your application does.

Optimizing Async Code for a Long-Running Operation

If your async code runs truly asynchronously, as we've seen, the largest overhead is the Post call to the calling SynchronizationContext, which causes a thread switch. As we discussed in "Choosing Not to Use SynchronizationContext" on page 51, you can use ConfigureAwait to opt out of that Post, to avoid paying the cost of the thread switch until it's really necessary. If your code is called in the WPF UI thread, it can be useful to avoid the repeated Posts.

The other context of the calling thread, captured by the ExecutionContext class, is also a source of overhead when writing async methods. As we saw in the section "Context" on page 27, .NET will capture and restore the ExecutionContext at every await. If you don't use ExecutionContext, the process of capturing and restoring the default context is heavily optimized, and very cheap. If you use any of the contexts captured by ExecutionContext, it becomes much more expensive. So, avoid using CallContext, LogicalCallContext, or impersonation in async code to improve performance.

Async Versus Manual Asynchronous Code

If you have existing UI code, it probably avoids responsiveness problems by some form of manual asynchronous technique. There are a variety of possible approaches, including:

- Creating a new thread
- Using ThreadPool.QueueUserWorkItem to do the long-running work on a background thread
- Using a BackgroundWorker
- Consuming an asynchronous API manually

All approaches involve at least one transfer back to the UI thread to present the result to the user, in the same way that async does automatically. In some of these approaches, this is implicit (for example, the RunWorkerCompleted event of BackgroundWorker), while in some, you need to explicitly call a BeginInvoke method.

The difference in speed between these approaches is relatively small, apart from creating a new thread, which is much slower. Async is at least as fast as any of them, if you avoid ExecutionContext. In fact, I find it a few percent faster than any other approach.

Because it's slightly faster, and because the code is more readable, I would always use async in preference to any of these techniques.

Async Versus Blocking Without a Long-Running Operation

A very common situation is to write a method that can take a long time occasionally, but is very fast 99% of the time. One example is a network request with a cache, where most requests can be served from the cache. The choice of whether to use async code for this kind of operation could be dependent on the overhead in the common case when the code completes synchronously rather than the overhead in the 1% of cases where it actually uses the asynchronous network operation.

Remember that the `await` keyword won't actually pause the method when it doesn't need to, in case it is given a `Task` that is already complete. The method containing that `await` can then also finish synchronously, in turn returning a `Task` that is already complete. In that way, entire chains of async methods can run synchronously.

Async methods, even when they run synchronously, are inevitably slower than their non-async equivalents. And now, there's no advantage to be gained through resources being released. The so-called async method isn't asynchronous, and the so-called blocking method doesn't block. However, the advantages of being asynchronous in the 1% of cases that the cache can't serve the request could be so large that it's worth writing async code anyway.

It all depends on how much slower async code is than non-async code, when they both return synchronously from a cache.

Again, this is really hard to measure accurately, because it depends so much on the situation. I find that calling an empty async method is 10 times slower than calling an empty non-async method.

It sounds slower than the non-async code, but remember, this is just the overhead. It will almost always be dominated by the actual work you're doing. For example, a lookup in a `Dictionary<string, string>` also costs around the same as 10 empty method calls.

Optimizing Async Code Without a Long-Running Operation

The overhead of an async method that completes synchronously, about 10 times the cost of an empty non-async method, comes from a few different places. Most of it is inevitable—for example, running the compiler-generated code, making its calls to the framework, and losing optimizations that are impossible because of the exception handling behavior of async methods.

The largest avoidable part of the overhead is the allocation of objects on the heap. It is very cheap to actually allocate an object. However, allocating more objects means the garbage collector needs to run more often, and it is expensive for an object to still be in use during a garbage collection.

The async machinery is designed to allocate as few objects as possible. That's why the state machine is a struct, as are the AsyncTaskMethodBuilder types. They are only moved to the heap if the async method is paused.

Task is not a struct, however, so it always needs to be allocated on the heap. For this reason, .NET has a few preallocated Tasks that are used when an async method completes synchronously, and returns one of a few common values, for example:

- A non-generic, successfully completed Task
- A Task<bool> containing true or false
- A Task<int> containing a small number
- A Task<T> containing null

If you are writing a cache that needs to have very high performance, and none of these apply, you can avoid the allocation by caching the completed Task rather than the value. It's rarely worthwhile, though, as you are likely to be allocating objects elsewhere in the code anyway.

So, in conclusion, async methods that finish synchronously are already very fast, and optimizing them further is hard. Only consider spending effort on caching Tasks if your application isn't as fast as you'd like, and you find that garbage collection is the issue.

Async Performance Summary

While async code always uses more processor time than the equivalent synchronous code, the difference is usually small in comparison to the operation that you're making asynchronous. In server-side code, the cost needs to be weighed against the memory footprint of the extra threads. In UI code, and when using actors for parallelism, async code is both faster and neater than implementing asynchronous patterns manually, so we should always use it.

Finally, when an operation usually completes immediately, there is no harm in using async code, because it is only slightly slower than the equivalent non-async code.

About the Author

Alex Davies is a coder, blogger, and concurrency enthusiast from England. He is currently a developer and product owner at Red Gate, working on tools for .NET developers. Before that, he completed a degree in computer science at Cambridge University, and still has theoretical CS in his blood. In his spare time, he writes an open source Actors framework for .NET, to let people write parallel programs more easily.

Have it your way.

O'Reilly eBooks

- Lifetime access to the book when you buy through oreilly.com
- Provided in up to four DRM-free file formats, for use on the devices of your choice:
  PDF, .epub, Kindle-compatible .mobi, and Android .apk
- Fully searchable, with copy-and-paste and print functionality
- Alerts when files are updated with corrections and additions

oreilly.com/ebooks/

Safari Books Online

- Access the contents and quickly search over 7000 books
  on technology, business, and certification guides
- Learn from expert video tutorials, and
  explore thousands of hours of video
  on technology and design topics
- Download whole books or chapters
  in PDF format, at no extra cost,
  to print or read on the go
- Get early access to books as they're being written
- Interact directly with authors of upcoming books
- Save up to 35% on O'Reilly print books

See the complete Safari Library at safari.oreilly.com

O'REILLY®

Get even more
for your money.

Join the O'Reilly Community, and register the O'Reilly books you own. It's free, and you'll get:

- $4.99 ebook upgrade offer
- 40% upgrade offer on O'Reilly print books
- Membership discounts on books and events
- Free lifetime updates to ebooks and videos
- Multiple ebook formats, DRM FREE
- Participation in the O'Reilly community
- Newsletters
- Account management
- 100% Satisfaction Guarantee

Signing up is easy:

1. **Go to: oreilly.com/go/register**
2. **Create an O'Reilly login.**
3. **Provide your address.**
4. **Register your books.**

Note: English-language books only

To order books online:
oreilly.com/store

For questions about products or an order:
orders@oreilly.com

To sign up to get topic-specific email announcements and/or news about upcoming books, conferences, special offers, and new technologies:
elists@oreilly.com

For technical questions about book content:
booktech@oreilly.com

To submit new book proposals to our editors:
proposals@oreilly.com

O'Reilly books are available in multiple DRM-free ebook formats. For more information:
oreilly.com/ebooks

O'REILLY®

Spreading the knowledge of innovators   oreilly.com